WHEN THE TIME HAD
FULLY COME

PATHWAY BOOKS
A SERIES OF CONTEMPORARY EVANGELICAL STUDIES

BIOGRAPHICAL NOTE

DR. HERMAN N. RIDDERBOS has distinguished himself on the continent for his work in the field of New Testament study. In 1936 he qualified for his doctor's title with a dissertation on the Sermon on the Mount. Among his notable publications are a commentary on Matthew (in two volumes), a large work on the Kingdom of God, a brief study of Paul and Jesus, and a commentary on Galatians. This latter commentary has been translated into English and appears in The New International Commentary on the New Testament series. Before he occupied the chair of New Testament at the Kampen Theological Seminary in 1943, Dr. Ridderbos was a pastor for eight years.

WHEN THE TIME HAD FULLY COME

STUDIES IN NEW TESTAMENT THEOLOGY

BY

HERMAN N. RIDDERBOS, TH.D.

*Professor of New Testament
in the Theological Seminary
at Kampen, The Netherlands*

WM. B. EERDMANS PUBLISHING CO.

GRAND RAPIDS   MICHIGAN

WHEN THE TIME HAD FULLY COME

by

HERMAN N. RIDDERBOS

COPYRIGHT 1957, BY WILLIAM B. EERDMANS PUBLISHING CO.

Set up and printed April 1957

LIBRARY OF CONGRESS CATALOG CARD NUMBER: 57-9772

The quotations of Scripture are from the American Standard Version and from the Revised Standard Version.

PRINTED IN THE UNITED STATES OF AMERICA

GENERAL INTRODUCTION

PATHWAY BOOKS, of which the present volume is the third to appear, are designed to help teachers, students, preachers, and laymen keep themselves informed on the important subjects and the crucial problems which confront the Christian church today. They are designed to help the reader bear witness to the Christian faith in the modern world.

The aim of Pathway Books is threefold:

(1) to give the latest results of research and reflection by leading evangelical scholars;

(2) to make relevant to modern man the basic affirmations of the Christian faith through a consideration of those questions which have come to the foreground of the modern scene; for example:

— what is the task of the Christian and the Church in modern secular society?

— what challenge does Communism present to Christianity?

— is there a conflict between the findings of modern science and the Bible?

— what is the nature of Biblical authority, and what authority does the Bible have?

— what contributions has the science of archeology made to the study of the Bible?

— what do modern history and culture reveal about the nature of man?

— what are the modern alternatives to Christianity?

— what is the spirit of the times?

— what is Barthianism, and at what points does it differ from Orthodoxy?

— what is the true place and function of liturgy in the Church?

- how is the Church to think Christologically? eschatologically?
- what is the practical significance of these areas of dogmatics?

(3) to display naked the idols of this age, and to urge upon modern man a thorough-going commitment to Christ and His gospel.

Consulting Editors for Pathway Books are: F. F. Bruce, Head of the Department of Biblical History and Literature, University of Sheffield, England, and Editor of *The Evangelical Quarterly;* Leon Morris, Vice-Principal of Ridley College, Melbourne, Australia; Bernard Ramm, Director of Graduate Studies in Religion, Baylor University, Waco, Texas; and Edward J. Young, Professor of Old Testament, Westminster Theological Seminary, Philadelphia, Pennsylvania.

The writer of each volume is, of course, solely responsible for the opinions and judgments expressed in his book. The Consulting Editors give valuable suggestions and advice, but the choice of subject and author, and the general direction of the series is the responsibility of the publisher.

For additional Pathway Book titles see the back cover.

CONTENTS

CHAPTER ONE

THE KINGDOM OF GOD ACCORDING TO THE WITNESS OF THE SYNOPTIC GOSPELS

THE KINGDOM OF GOD, or the Kingdom of Heaven, is one of the most central concepts in the history of revelation. Prepared in the Old Testament, notably in the so-called enthronement Psalms and in the prophecies, it makes its appearance in the overture of the New Testament as the contents of the great proclamation of salvation, first of the herald, John the Baptist, then of Christ Himself: "The kingdom of God is at hand" (Mark 1:15). Especially in the Synoptic Gospels it remains in the foreground. It constitutes the nucleus of Christ's parables, indeed of His entire mission and message. In John and Paul, however, it seems to withdraw. But this is only seemingly so, as I hope to show in detail in connection with Paul. And the conclusion of the New Testament, the Apocalypse of John, is connected with the beginning, inasmuch as in it the great antithesis between the Kingdom of God and the powers of the world is forcibly and dramatically expressed in all its fullness. So it can be established that the New Testament as a whole is the book of the revelation of the Kingdom of God.

It cannot be said with the same stress that in the consciousness of the Church and in the history of theology the concept of the Kingdom of God always has held such a central place. The old Church, it is true, at first lived for some time in the expectation of the early return of Christ. And the great Father of the

Church, Augustine, in his imposing work *De Civitate Dei,* at the decline of the Roman Empire, again placed the great struggle between the two realms in the center. But in his book there was also the foundation for the Roman Catholic doctrine that the Kingdom of God in her earthly manifestation coincides with the Church. Thus, in Catholicism the Church gradually superseded the Kingdom of God, and the Kingdom of God has today disappeared behind the impressive facades of the Catholic cathedrals.

It is true that in Reformed theology a great change occurred on this point. Particularly in Calvin the idea of the sovereignty of God was the central point of view of theology. And for this theocentric character of Calvin's theology the idea of the Kingdom of God was naturally an important one. Still it cannot be said that the Reformers were typically Kingdom-of-God theologians. Their viewpoint was theocentric, but in a rather static manner. The historical and eschatological aspects of the biblical revelation of the Kingdom of God were not prominent in their theology.

The great theological discussions about the concept of the Kingdom of God, as we know them in our own days, date in fact from the nineteenth century. The liberal school, for instance, thought they could appeal, for their concept of the Christian faith, to Christ's preaching of the Kingdom. They contended that they called for a return from Paul to Christ, and from the doctrines of the Church to what they called the simple, spiritual gospel of Christ. To them the Kingdom of God was the realm of love and peace that was founded by Jesus on earth, and which man is to extend. It is worthy of notice that especially in America the social aspect of the Kingdom of God thus interpreted came most to the foreground, whereas the liberal theology in Europe stressed the individual, personal significance of it as first and foremost. But whether the religious personality or the new social order was placed in the center, the Kingdom of God was an idea which was strongly oriented to the *Aufklarung,* and which agreed with the optimistic view of life presented by evolutionism.

In Europe this theology held its own until World War I. Then the older peoples of the Continent, proud of their culture, found that the blindfold with which they had covered their eyes was plucked away. And from that time dates, in theology, the great influence of the eschatological concept of the Kingdom of God.

In the exegesis of the New Testament the discovery had indeed been made earlier that the liberal portrait of Jesus and the liberal concept of the Kingdom of God could neither historically nor biblically be maintained. Johannes Weisz and Albert Schweitzer had shown that the concept of the Kingdom of Heaven originated from a world different from that of the *Aufklarung,* namely, from the world of the late Jewish apocalypses. And Albert Schweitzer in particular had, in his so-called "consistent eschatology," sought to explain the entire gospel and the entire history of Jesus from this eschatological viewpoint. Jesus, he said, was expecting the immediate entry of the Eschaton. He was not a moralist, but an apocalypticus. His commandments are not meant to hold good for all times but for the very end of time, in which the world will have reached its final phase. They contain eschatological ethics, interim ethics. And Jesus' life would have been — in the opinion of Schweitzer — one continual expectation of the entrance of the Eschaton, an expectation which has never been realized and which ended in Jesus' death on the cross.

Schweitzer's fantastic concept of the life of Jesus has not been followed. It asks a too drastic readjustment of the history of the Gospels. Yet his eschatological interpretation of the Kingdom of God was reverted to when the supremacy of facts had shown the failure of the liberal theology. Many people began to understand then again that the Kingdom of God is a transcendental entity, that it is beyond the power of man and that it represents a new and other world, the world of God. And the gospel began to be read with new eyes.

Thus, although we can say that there is, in this respect, a new and better understanding of the gospel, when it is recognized that the Kingdom of God is primarily a transcendental entity, and that it contains the acts of God, a new controversy has arisen about the nature of these acts. For although it is admitted that the Kingdom of God in the gospel is an eschatological entity, this does not imply that the biblical representation of this eschatology is considered as acceptable and valid for the modern man. What does eschatology really mean? What is the underlying, existential significance of this concept? These questions are asked in present-day theological discussion again and again. I have only to recall the theme of the meeting of the World Council of Churches at Evanston, 1954. What does it mean that Christ is the hope of the world? It is the question concerning the essential nature of the eschatology and of the future of the Kingdom of God. Here, in fact, the old contrast comes to the fore again. Is the Kingdom of God and is the coming of Christ only to be thought of in a spiritual way, as a reality which is only experienced as a divine, sanctifying, and renewing force? Or is the Kingdom of God also transcendental in the sense that God will replace the present world by a different one, the world of the resurrection from the dead, the world of the new heavens and of the new earth?

It seems to me that in Evanston the struggle was especially waged between the representatives of a more biblical, European theology on the one hand, and the representatives of typical American modernism on the other. In the Europe of our day, however, a no less fierce controversy is raging both over the essences of eschatology and over the nature of the coming of God in His kingdom. Here it is the personality of R. Bultmann which has reshaped the old modernism into a new form and which has a great influence, more particularly on German theology. About him I should like to say one or two things more.

Bultmann agrees with the criticism of the old liberal concept of the Kingdom of God. No doubt, he says, what matters in the Kingdom of God is the history of the acts of God, and not the realization of the kingdom by man. The question must be raised, however, he says, how we have to understand these acts of God. Is this a heavenly impact on the natural world order? Is this the belief in miracles which have happened, and which are still to happen? No modern man, he contends, can in that sense believe in miracles any longer. The Kingdom of God leaves the natural world order intact. Neither does it mean an intervention, from the outside, into the human mind, such as a supernatural rebirth. We should, he says, discover the real, lasting significance in these mythical concepts. And this significance is not of a cosmic, but of an existential nature. God has dealings with man, and He deals with man again and again. God acts by addressing him in the gospel, and by speaking to him of a possibility over which man himself has no disposal and in favor of which he is to make his choice by faith. Only then will man be redeemed, and his redemption is identical with his real existence. So long as man is seeking support and a foothold in the world which he controls, through the possibilities that lie within his reach, he is not an "essential man," he is not truly free, and he does not exist as man.

In Christ's Cross, Bultmann argues, God showed us a different possibility, namely, the possibility to choose in favor of that which lies outside human reach. In this way, that is, in showing and choosing this possibility, Jesus has become the Christ, that is, the Savior and Lord of man. In this way we must look upon belief in the resurrection as belief in the salvation significance of His Cross. And if we really are to become free, we shall have to be crucified with Christ, and to die with Him in this way. So the coming of God in Christ is, consequently, nothing but this, that God, in the gospel, again and again, places us before this existential decision. There is no such thing as the history of redemption in the sense of a continuous revelation of the Kingdom resulting in the coming of Christ. That is a mythological way of putting it. There is only a history of salvation in the existential sense of the word, namely, as a succession of personal, human decisions in response to the actual speaking of God in the gospel.

*   *   *

Returning from these interpretations of the Kingdom of God to our starting point, namely, to the proclamation of the Kingdom in the Synoptic Gospels, we should first of all definitely establish that the exhortation both of Jesus and John the Baptist: Repent, for the Kingdom of Heaven is at hand, can only be understood as part of the great prophetic, eschatological tradition of old Israel. Kingdom of Heaven, *malkoeth shamaim,* as the term is used in later Jewry, is the standard expression for the world of God's redemption as it was promised by the prophets, and in a variety of forms, both national and apocalyptic, was expected in Israel. The new element in the preaching of John and Jesus, then, was not that they spoke of the Kingdom of Heaven, but that they proclaimed its being at hand. It was an eschatological blast on the trumpet.

At the same time, however, it should be stated at this point — and this is no less important for defining the concept of the Kingdom of Heaven — that Christ's appearance and preaching in no way seemed to answer to this eschatological character of the Kingdom. That is the difference between Jesus and John, and that is John's problem: "Art thou he that cometh, or look we for another?" (Matt. 11:2). For Jesus does not come with a winnowing fork in His hand, but He walks the land as a physician. He blesses the poor in spirit, and He teaches in the Sermon on the Mount that we have to love our enemies and that we must take no thought for the morrow. Is this preaching the Kingdom? Schweitzer said that the Sermon on the Mount is interim ethics. But nobody can believe this to be true. For Jesus, in His radical commandments, does not appeal to the fact that the Day of the Lord is at hand and that consequently all earthly interests no longer count for anything, but to the fact that God maketh His sun to rise on the evil and on the good, and that

He takes care of the birds and the flowers. What has this to do with eschatology?

Of late years this particular characteristic of Christ's eschatology has again been in the limelight. The recently found Dead Sea Scrolls give us an insight into the nature of Jewish sects in the days of Jesus. In these sects, too, there was a burning eschatological longing and so there are those who think that they can show the existence of a connection between John's and Christ's appearance, and these sects. I may remind you, for instance, of the publications of the French scholar Dupont-Sommer, who sees a forerunner of Jesus in the "teacher of righteousness" who appears in these Dead Sea Scrolls and who plays an eschatological part in them. On examination of this sect-eschatology, however, as expressed for example in these Dead Sea Scrolls, one finds an immense difference. War against enemies, wild battle scenes and victory constitute the expectation here, in a hardly distinguishable coincidence of national and apocalyptical features. Turning to the Gospels, however, the first great example of Christ's preaching the Kingdom of God is the Sermon on the Mount, and in it we find the radical demand for love and for reliance on God.

Too little notice has also been taken of the fact that Christ Himself purposely and emphatically deals with the manner in which the Kingdom comes. Especially the parables of the Kingdom in Matthew 13 and Mark 4, the parable of the sower, the parable of the tares among the wheat, and the parable of the seed growing automatically are very significant for the right understanding of Jesus' preaching of the Kingdom. What is the point of these parables?

In the interpretation of the parable of the sower the stress is mostly laid on the different ways in which the word of God can be heard. And this also belongs undoubtedly to the contents of the parable. But one just misses the tenor if one sees in it a timeless exhortation to take the preaching of the gospel to heart. For in these parables Jesus reveals to His disciples the nature of the Kingdom of God. He teaches them how to know the

mysteries of the Kingdom. What mystery is it? This, before anything else, that the eschatological Kingdom of God is coming as
a seed, seemingly the weakest and most defenseless thing there
is. It can be devoured by the fowls, it can be choked by the
thorns, it can be scorched by the sun, and sometimes it can
hardly be distinguished from the tares. That is the secret of the
Kingdom. And back of this lies an even greater mystery, namely,
that He who brings the Kingdom is a Sower, seemingly the most
dependent of men. "A Sower went forth to sow" and "He who
sows the good seed is the Son of Man" — that is the great
mystery of the Kingdom of God.

So far it may look as if the liberal theology with its spiritual
concept of the Kingdom had a better understanding of Jesus
than all who, later, placed all emphasis on the eschatological
character. Yet appearances are deceptive here. For behind this
secrecy of the Kingdom the entire dynamic power of God's great
deeds is concealed. That is already pointed out in the parables
themselves. They are not only about sowing, but also about
harvesting, and the harvest is also in the parables (in spite of
C. H. Dodd), the eschatological harvest in the future. But above
all things, this power lies hidden in the person of Jesus Himself.
The humble and unobtrusive figure of the Sower covers the
hidden greatness of Christ's Messiahship. That is the real mystery of the Kingdom. This hidden greatness of Jesus Christ is,
strictly speaking, the subject of the Gospels, and it is this greatness which determines the nature of the Kingdom.

The great liberal theologian Adolf von Harnack said, it is
true, that the gospel of the Kingdom is the gospel of the Father,
and not of the Son. And many people have repeated it after him.
But here, indeed, lies the great error of the liberal portrait of
Jesus and the liberal concept of the Kingdom of God. For the
character and the purport of the Kingdom is determined by the
person and by the way of Jesus. He is the *auto-basileia,* as
Origen expressed it. And thus in his earthly life there is that
curious tension between revelation and mystery, between eschatological greatness and human weakness. To the first belongs the

authority *(exousia)*, with which He speaks in the Sermon on the Mount, and with which He forgives sins on earth. To this belong His miracles, the signals of the great time of salvation. But at the same time He forbids men to make them known. His Messiahship is a secret. The whole paradox of it is concentrated in the name Son of Man, that is, human being amidst human beings, man who sows, and who must bide the result of the harvest. But it also implies: Son of Man who, according to the prophecy of Daniel 7, receives all power from the hands of the Most High. It is in Him that God works His great deeds, for this Son of Man is under the law of the divine "must," of the *dein* and *prepein* as it says in the New Testament.

That is why the Cross, too, is part of the revelation of the Kingdom, for the Son of Man *must* go to Jerusalem. The order of the divine work of redemption demands this. Nowhere is the mystery of the Kingdom more profound than in the Cross of Jesus. The Sower becomes, Himself, the seed. But at the same time an eschatological process is taking place. The dimension of the Kingdom becomes visible already in the signs attending Christ's death and affecting nature. Above all it becomes manifest in His resurrection. Then the Son of Man strides along to His great future, and He is given the power which Daniel 7 mentions. In Christ the Kingdom is breaking through the boundaries of the earthly category, and what was heard in the ear, that is preached upon the housetops (Matt. 10:27).

That is the concept of the Kingdom in the Synoptic Gospels. It is one of presence as well as of futurity, of both secrecy and revelation. The rising of Christ marks the boundary. In it the two aeons coincide, as it were. It belongs to the presence of the Kingdom. For it has taken place upon the earth. The Eschaton has come in Christ. The world has been opened for the Kingdom of God. The strong one has been overcome in his own house. But the resurrection belongs to the future as well. The risen Savior no longer belongs to the earthly category. He is the First-fruits of the great future. But the final phase, the new heaven and the new earth, is yet to come. First the seed must be sown, then not only Israel but all the world must live in the dispensation and under the responsibility of that which has been seen and heard in Christ.

In the Synoptic Gospels the present and the future significance of the Kingdom largely coincide. Before the resurrection of Christ the perspectives are often very unclear, in accordance with the nature of the prophecy. Mention is made of the appearance of the Son of Man and of the Kingdom in glory as of an event that can be expected at once. Mention is made of the latter days within the frame of the Jewish land. It is as if everything converges upon one point, resurrection and parousia, and as if, on Christ's departing from the earth, the full revelation of the Kingdom can already be expected. But the resurrection opens up a new perspective. It teaches us to distinguish between what has come, and what is to come. It is the starting-point of a new dispensation in the future of the Kingdom.

*   *   *

In the light of all this we come to understand something of the mystery of the Kingdom of God in history. The Kingdom of God does not primarily mean the end of history; and expecting the Kingdom of God does not in the first place mean busying ourselves with the things of the last day. The Kingdom of God enters into history. The parable of the Sower continues to be crucial, and the warning addressed to the laborers who wanted to root up the tares among the wheat has remained valid to this day. All this must be pointed out to sectarianism and to every theology or view of life which does not take the presence of the Kingdom into account. Because the Kingdom of God has entered into this world, we must say that this world is full of the redemptive power of God. For the Cross of Christ was placed in this world, and Christ arose *here*. It is this effective power that forms the subject matter of the parables of the mustard seed and the leaven. The former deals with the expansive power of the Kingdom. The seed is very small but the tree becomes very great, the birds lodge in its branches and people seek shelter under its leaves. The Kingdom does not keep aloof from the world, but is seeking it and its wide relationships. It is seeking the peoples, and the ends of the earth. That is its extent. But it is also like a leaven that is leavening the whole. That is its intensity. It penetrates all the relations, all the fields of life. That is why eschatologism — that is, an undue stress upon eschatology — is as unbiblical as the connection of the Kingdom with the immanence philosophy. Eschatologism misjudges the resurrection, and the power of the exalted Lord through His Word and Spirit. It disregards the fact that the field into which the seed must be sown is the world. And that Christ, for that reason, is the hope of *this* world.

But this presence of the Kingdom is, so to speak, surrounded by the future. And the presence of the Kingdom is felt only in so far as it is carried and governed by the future. Here the Christian faith, here biblical theology has to wage a mortal battle against secularization, and against the humanization of the Kingdom of God. Both are unbiblical and, in a sense, un-Christian, because they place creation and nature as a self-contained entity against God and the Kingdom. The Kingdom in this view does come into the world and into man, but merely in a spiritual sense. The law of nature, the closed world-order of which man is, in his natural existence, part and parcel, lies beyond the control of the Kingdom. Here the resurrection has become an idea, the mythological way of putting a spiritual reality; here the future of Jesus Christ has disappeared from view; here Christ is no longer in the all-embracing sense the hope of the world, namely, in this sense that He will also renew creation and will cause life to break forth from death.

I am thinking of the secularization of the Kingdom of God, for instance, in American theology; I am also thinking of the existentialist interpretation of the gospel after the manner of Bultmann. Here the theocentric viewpoint has disappeared. Here only that is left of the transcendence of the Kingdom which is necessary to make man truly man. Thus the Kingdom is the liberty which makes man free as a spiritual being. This liberty must come from the other side, from God's, through man's being addressed by the Word of God. That is the transcendence. But this transcendence is restricted to that which makes a man really into man in the sense of existentialist philosophy. God is God only insofar as He is necessary to the realization of this man. God exists *sub specie hominis*. That is the God of existentialism. That is the humanization of the Kingdom of God in the individualistic sense of the word.

In contrast to this there is the impressive concept of the Kingdom of God in the Gospels. God is the Lord of creation who makes His Kingdom to come in His Son Jesus Christ. He is not helpless against a so-called closed world-order. That is why God raises Him from the dead. And that is why Christ is the hope of the world, and why the Kingdom that came is only the announcement of the Kingdom that is to come. And that is why the Church of today is living in the interim between the great times of Christ. The resurrection of Christ is casting its light in two directions. It is the proof of what has happened, and the guarantee or pledge of what will happen. This is the deep sense of the alternation between perfect and future tenses in the Synoptic Gospels and throughout the New Testament.

*   *   *

I referred to the Church before. The Church also belongs to the revelation of the Kingdom. It derives its existence and the mode of its existence from the Kingdom of God. For this reason the relation between Kingdom of God and Church must also be discussed at this point.

It is often denied that the Church also belongs to the revelation of the Kingdom. Jesus, it is thought, was the prophet of the Kingdom and not of the Church. In the Gospels the word *basileia* occurs on almost every page. But the Church is only mentioned twice altogether in the three Gospels, namely, in the well-known statements of Matthew 16: "Upon this rock I will build my church," and of Matthew 18:17: "If he [the sinner] refuse to hear them [the two or three witnesses] tell it unto the church." But, as many scholars have maintained for a long time, these two statements are quite "lost" (isolated) in the gospel, and will therefore have to be looked upon as "church-theology." The Kingdom, they assert, is divine and spiritual. The Church is a sociological phenomenon. It has no inner relationship with the Kingdom.

We may call it a fortunate symptom that in contemporary theology the Church is more and more coming to the fore again, and that in the so-called theology of the New Testament, too, the connection between the Kingdom and the Church, *basileia* and *ekklēsia,* is once more fully accentuated. Their connection is, indeed, in the light of what I said above, absolutely incontestable and in my opinion the New Testament concept of the Church can only be approached in a fully adequate way from the Kingdom of God. The fact that the word *ekklēsia* does not come to the forefront in the Gospels should not deceive us, because from the very first there appears, in the Kingdom of God preached by Jesus, with increasing clarity of outline, a people. The concept has its preformation in old Israel, in the people of the covenant and of the promises. In the Gospels it can, therefore, without any further announcement or description, be called *ekklēsia.* For *ekklēsia* in the New Testament is not a new word or a new concept. It is, indeed, nothing but the translation of *kahal,* already current in the Septuagint, denoting the Old Testament people of God, the congregation of Israel. The new thing is that this *ekklēsia* now comes into the light of the Kingdom of God. All earlier qualifications of the *ekklēsia* as the people of the election, of the covenant and of the promises, are sublimated in the Kingdom of God, are "fulfilled" as it says in the New Testament. When the Kingdom comes, the proper and *spiritual* sense of the Church comes into the light. But in the *extensive* sense, too, the *ekklēsia* acquires in the Kingdom new proportions and new relations. The *ekklēsia* is integrated in the worldwide power of the Kingdom: henceforth it is foregathered from all nations. This is the one great line connecting *basileia* and *ekklēsia*. So one can speak, in a sense, of the eschatological character of the Church, of its being concerned in God's acts of salvation in His Son Jesus Christ.

But this main connection is intersected and further determined by another, namely, by the relation between the Messiah and the Church. For the Messiah is the King of the people of the future, He is the Shepherd, sent by God to gather His flock. Therefore Jesus blesses the poor in spirit as the Old Testament people of God, who hunger and thirst after the righteousness that will prevail in the Kingdom of God. But He also calls, in His twelve apostles, the fullness of the new Israel. There is, more, however. Not before the Kingdom comes does it appear in what an unexpected way the Messiah links Himself with the *ekklēsia*. He is not only the founder of the *ekklēsia,* but He identifies Himself with it. The Gospels give a double concept of this, namely, that of the Son of Man, and that of the Servant of Jahweh. But in both concepts the leading thought is that the Messiah represents the *ekklēsia* in His own person. He represents it as the Son of Man, who, as you remember, received in Daniel 7 the kingship for the benefit of the holy people of the Most High. And He represents it as the Servant of Jahweh, who for His people's sake is given up in the judgment of God. The two figures of the Son of Man and of the Servant of Jahweh form a wonderful unity in the Gospels. But the Messiah is always the representative of the *ekklēsia*. Nowhere is the significance of this more profound than in the Passion, which, in all its soberness and sublimity, is the history of the Messiah with His *ekklēsia*. Time and again it has been said that the idea of the vicarious atonement is a *corpus alienum* in the original gospel. More serious a mistake can hardly be made, not only because of the unity of the New Testament, but primarily because the gospel of the Kingdom itself contains this hidden kernel.

Consequently it can be said that these three ideas — of the Kingdom, of the Messiah, and of the *ekklēsia* — formed an integrated unity in the original gospel. The eschatological, the Christological, and the ecclesiological point of view are never separable in the preaching of the Kingdom. There is no Kingdom without the Messiah, the Son of Man, the Servant of the Lord. And there is no Messiah without the *ekklēsia* which He represents in His subjection to the curse and in His exaltation, in His death, and in His resurrection. That is why Jesus speaks of *my ekklēsia* (Matt. 16:18), that is why He can "give his life a ransom for many" (Mark 10:45), that is why He can also appoint the Kingdom to His *ekklēsia,* as the Father has appointed it unto Him (Luke 22:29).

*   *   *

One may ask, What is the practical meaning of all this for the Church in the present time? I would like to make three brief remarks concerning this.

First: The Church as the Church of the Kingdom stands and falls with the reality of the great deeds of God in Jesus Christ both in the fullness of time and in the great future. For surely the Church, too, is included in them. Should this history of salvation cease to exist in past or future, then the Church as the Church of the Kingdom ceases to exist. So the first implication of all that has been said is that the Church, to prove its legitimacy, must be built on this foundation.

The legitimacy of the Church is one of the most important questions we are facing in the ecclesiastical problems of our time. It involves, too, the question of the unity of the Church. These questions cannot be answered in passing. But from the viewpoint of the Kingdom of God the questions of the legitimacy and of the unity of the Church will continue to find their answer in the conformity of the Church to its foundation in the history of the revelation. All of this has a bearing on the great principle of the apostolicity of the Church. For the Church is built on the apostolic testimony of the great deeds of God in Jesus Christ. The apostles are the plenipotentiary witnesses of Christ and the founders of the Church. Therefore the legitimacy and also the unity of the Church lie in its apostolicity. There is the true Church, and there is the true unity of the Church, where the Church is one with the apostles, for there the Church of the Kingdom reveals itself.

Second: all this touches the Church's own definition *of itself* in the light of the Kingdom of God. But the Kingdom of God also defines the Church in its relation to *the world*. The Church has a foundation of its own, has its own rules, its own mode of existence. But precisely because of the fact that it is the Church of the Kingdom, it has also a positive relation with the world, for the Kingdom of God is seeking acceptance in the world. A sower went forth to sow. And the field is the world. That is why the Church is seeking catholicity. And this catholicity has a double aspect, one of extension and one of intensity, in accordance with the nature of the Kingdom. So the Church is as wide as the world. The horizons of the world are also the horizons of the Church; therefore its urge to carry on missionary work, to emigrate, to cross frontiers. This is because the Church is the Church of the Kingdom. She is not allowed to be self-contained.

But there is also an intensive catholicity of the Church because of the Kingdom. The Church is related to life as a whole. It is not a drop of oil on troubled waters. It has a mission in this world and in the entire structure of the world. This statement does not arise from cultural optimism. This is the confession of the kingship of Christ. For this reason, too, the Church is the Church of the Kingdom.

And the third remark is my concluding one: as Church of the Kingdom, the Church is seeking the future. She has received her talents for the present. But her Lord who went into a far country will return. Her waiting for Him consists of working. Otherwise she will hear: What have you done with my talent?

But her working for Him consists in waiting also. All parables have the same issue: what will happen when the Lord comes and the harvest begins? In the tremendous world surrounding her, amidst all that she hears and sees, in the middle of temptations either to forget the present for the future, or heaven for the earth, she has to represent the picture of those who have trimmed their lamps and go forth to meet the bridegroom.

CHAPTER TWO

THE SIGNIFICANCE OF THE SERMON ON THE MOUNT

ONE OF THE most important and impressive phases in the teaching of Jesus on the Kingdom of Heaven is that which is known as the Sermon on the Mount, of which we have two different accounts, namely, Matthew 5-7 and Luke 6:20-49. The Matthean version is a more detailed and architectural construction than that of Luke. The distinction is especially noticeable in the great passage Matthew 5:17-48, where Jesus elucidates the law and presents His interpretation thereof in contrast with that of the scribes and Pharisees. Another point of difference is that Matthew gathers a lot of proverbial sayings and expressions in the Sermon on the Mount, while in Luke these are scattered and used on different occasions. The diverse accounts of the Sermon on the Mount present a problem, but I am not here concerned with the various details. It is, however, necessary to bear in mind the manner in which Matthew construes his Gospel. His manner is especially noticeable in the first half of the Gospel, where he arranges his material in accordance with a definite principle of composition. This can be seen, for instance, in his accumulation of identical material without a full recognition of chronology. In this way the beautiful composition was formed which we can admire in Chapters 4 through 9. Verses 12 through 25 of Chapter 4 reveal a general impression of the ministry of Jesus in Galilee. Matthew is describing Christ's journey through the country, His teaching in the synagogues and "preaching the gospel of the kingdom, and healing all manner of disease and all manner of sickness among the people"

(4:23). Chapters 5 through 7 record an extensive illustration of Christ's preaching of the gospel of the Kingdom, while Chapters 8 and 9 contain a summary of a number of Christ's miracles, which Mark records in a different way and order. This justifies the conclusion that Matthew construed these chapters in accordance with a literary principle; and it may give a partial explanation of the phenomenon, that the scattered presentation of words and sayings in Luke forms an impressive whole in Matthew.

We may say that what Jesus is told to have said on this special occasion on one of the Galilean hills in the presence of His disciples and a large crowd which followed Him, belongs, even from the viewpoint of literary composition, to the most beautiful and impressive part of His teaching of the Kingdom of God.

Indeed, it belongs to the most beautiful of His teaching. In this composition we come to learn the typical form of teaching which Jesus employed. It abounds in plastic splendor, it is sublime and yet in perfect harmony with ordinary and everyday existence. It is of such a nature that it contains those extraordinary, frequently paradoxical sayings, the so-called *meschalim,* intended to incite those listening to reflection and to which applies: "He that hath ears to hear, let him hear." In using this form of teaching Jesus associates Himself with rabbinical usage of His day. Parables, proverbs, unexpected and pointed sayings enjoyed special preference, as reference to rabbinical literature will show. In the teaching of Jesus, however, and explicitly so in the Sermon on the Mount, this form reaches the very pinnacle of splendor and a power of expression which is unsurpassed in Jewish literature. It is therefore not to be marveled at that a large number of the Lord's sayings in the Sermon on the Mount became common property in literature, even far beyond the limits of Christianity.

*   *   *

It is, however, not the form as an expression of beauty which causes the deepest impression, but the content. In his conclusion

to the Sermon Matthew describes the effect of these sayings of
Jesus on the multitudes thus: "When Jesus had finished these
words, the multitudes were astonished at his teaching: for he
taught them as one having authority, and not as their scribes"
(7:28). Even in this response of His listeners it appears that a
higher reality, co-existent with the Person of Jesus, became
apparent in His teaching. Here was not only an appeal to fore-
going authorities, as in the case of the scribes, nor only a
claim to a divine mission, as in the case of the prophets. Jesus
spoke from inherent power and authority. In contrast to the
Jewish teachers of law He presented His "But verily, I tell you,"
and at the end of the Sermon He even identified Himself with
the One who in the final world-judgment will demand an
account of all that men have done in their life on earth: "Not
everyone that saith unto me, Lord, Lord, shall enter the kingdom of heaven; but he that doeth the will of my Father who is
in heaven. Many will say to me in that day, Lord, Lord, did we
not prophesy by thy name? . . . . And then I will profess unto
them, I never knew you: depart from me, ye that work iniquity"
(7:21-23). It is clear from this that the Sermon on the Mount
is only to be understood when there is a full recognition of the
frame in which it appears, namely, the gospel of the Kingdom
of God and of His mighty deeds in His Son Jesus Christ.

The reality of the Kingdom of God in the Sermon manifests
itself in another way, which is no less the cause of the impressive-
ness of the Sermon. What I mean is the special *radicalism of its
commandments,* which lends this Sermon its own distinct
character, and which consists in the unsurpassed manner in
which Jesus gives expression to the command of love towards
God and towards one's neighbor. It is this same awe-inspiring
radicalism which, on another occasion, causes the disciples'
amazement and calls forth the question: "Who then can be
saved?" (Matt. 19:25). The many instances of this radicalism
require no attestation. I need only mention the way in which
Jesus speaks of marriage, of the non-resistance to evil, of love
towards enemies in Matthew 5:21-48. Concerning love towards

God, I would refer you to the absolute dilemma reflected in Matthew 6:24: "No man can serve two masters; for either he will hate the one, and love the other; or else he will hold to one, and despise the other." And the admonitions: "Lay not up for yourselves treasures upon the earth . . . but lay up for yourselves treasures in heaven . . . for where thy treasure is, there will thy heart be also," and, "Therefore I say unto you, Be not anxious for your life, what ye shall eat, or what ye shall drink . . ." (6:19, 20, 25).

In these sayings the religious and ethical demands are worked out to a consequence and depth which not only explain the remarkable impression which the Sermon must directly have created on its first hearers, but which also explain why subsequent hearers speak of the *problem* of the Sermon on the Mount, the problem of its purpose and purport as an ethical commandment, and the problem of its practicability.

*   *   *

The first question that must be considered is that of the relationship and connection between these absolute commands and the Kingdom of Heaven. Is the Sermon on the Mount positive proof for the liberal view of the Kingdom of God, because in it neither the eschatological environment of the gospel nor the alteration of the aeons stands in the foreground, but conversion of life in a personal and social sense? Is therefore the Kingdom of God, according to the Sermon on the Mount, mainly or exclusively a new moral and religious standard? Or should these absolute commands be seen as having an entirely different purpose, namely, to display the terms under which alone it is possible to enter the eschatological Kingdom? Or is here still another possibility, namely, that these conditions, because of their radicalism, intend to make it known that the entrance to the Kingdom of God cannot be gained by personal righteousness? In other words, should the Sermon on the Mount be understood merely as a mirror of the moral misery and incapability of man, in the same way in which Paul explains the law in Romans 7? All these interpretations of the Sermon on the Mount are found in the history of exegesis.

To my mind there are not sufficient grounds to defend the thesis that the exhortations of the Sermon have only such a negative tendency, namely, to make it clear that nobody is able to meet the demands of God and to bar the road of self-righteousness for a sinner. In favor of this view commentators have appealed sometimes to Matthew 5:20, where Jesus says: "For I say unto you, that except your righteousness shall exceed the righteousness of the scribes and Pharisees, ye shall in no wise enter into the kingdom of heaven"; or to Matthew 5:48: "Ye therefore shall [must] be perfect, as your heavenly Father is perfect." The appeal to these texts, however, is inadmissible. When Jesus demanded from His disciples that their righteousness should exceed that of the scribes and Pharisees, He did not confront them with this demand in such a way as to denote that the righteousness of the scribes is so very perfect that to excel it would be an impossibility. On the contrary, the entire teaching of Jesus is full of criticism of the emptiness and worthlessness of the righteousness of the scribes. And as for Matthew 5:48, Jesus does not, in any universal sense, demand of man moral equality with God. The word "perfect" as used here denotes quite a different meaning. It concerns the "perfectness," the consistency of *love*. Man is bound not only to love his neighbor but also his enemies. It is in this sense that the heavenly Father, too, is perfect. "For he maketh his sun to rise on the evil and the good, and sendeth rain on the just and the unjust" (Matt. 5:45). There is no room in His love for half measures. Hence perfect love is also demanded from His children, not partial, not only towards friends, but enemies as well. Hence also Luke can add in the corresponding passage in his Gospel: "Be ye merciful, even as your Father is merciful" (Luke 6:36). "Even as" means "equally perfect," "equally consistent." Therefore, it is not possible to appeal to this to contend the positive tenor of the law in the Sermon on the Mount. It belongs to the essential quality, I might well say to the *logic* of the Kingdom of the Heavens, that a disciple of Jesus does not content himself with love merely towards his fellows. There is no question of straining the moral demands *ad absurdum*.

More, however, must be mentioned. No doubt, Jesus makes obedience to His commands a condition for the entry into the Kingdom. It constitutes the narrow gate, the hard way that leads to life. Yet Jesus does not speak about this obedience to His commands and about the entry into the Kingdom in the form of a mere *conditionalis*. He asserts this obedience also in a positive sense, in the form of an indicative. The Sermon on the Mount opens with the beatitudes, the proclaiming of salvation to the poor in spirit, to the poor and destitute people of God who hopefully expect the revelation of the Kingdom. And to them Jesus proclaims clearly and distinctly, speaks in a positive and definitive manner: "You are the light of the world, you are the salt of the earth. . . . Let your light so shine before men, that they may see your good works, and give glory to your father who is in heaven."

Herein is revealed the *ordo salutis* of the Kingdom of Heaven. The scheme of Jewish soteriology is hereby dissolved. No longer is salvation only in heaven and in the future, nor can this future salvation only be earned by moral exertion. No, the Son of Man has come for the redemption of sins *on earth*. He introduces the future salvation to the present. Accordingly the beatification is valid here and now: Blessed are the poor in spirit, for theirs *is* the Kingdom of Heaven. That is the light which came to shine on earth, and that is the light in which the disciples may rejoice. For that reason they are called the light of the world, not primarily because of what they *do*, but what they *receive*. But that light must beam forth, for men do not light a lamp and put it under a bushel. What Jesus thus requires is that men reflect the light which they received from Him. The endowment of the Kingdom accomplishes good works in its recipients, and thus the Kingdom finds embodiment in the lives of the faithful.

It is the great reality of the future which in Jesus Christ has come to earth which also touches those belonging to Him. That is the order of the beatitudes and commandments. In this way the commandments can also be a conditional expression of admittance to the Kingdom. Whosoever fails to radiate the love of Christ thereby proves that he has no part in Christ and is not included in the Kingdom of God. He also has no part in the Kingdom to come. Yet this does not imply that God's bestowal is preceded by human effort. The order of things is quite the contrary. Jesus explains to us this order in the beautiful account of the woman who was a sinner (Luke 7:36-50). This woman displayed her love for Jesus excessively and the Pharisees were astonished and shook their heads. Jesus then narrated to them the story of the two debtors and asked which of the two debtors would love the creditor most. The answer must be: "He . . . whom he forgave the most." In conclusion Jesus replies to both the Pharisees and the woman: "Wherefore I say unto thee, Her sins, which are many, are forgiven; for she loved much; but to whom little is forgiven, the same loveth little." Observe the order: Jesus does not say: *because* she loved much, I forgive her sins. On the contrary, He means to say: it is possible to conclude from the greatness of her love that her numerous sins have been forgiven, even as the slender love of the Pharisees discloses that little has been forgiven them. "To whom little is forgiven, the same loveth little." This is the application of the parable of the two debtors, and is the order of the Kingdom of Heaven.

This order also accounts for the radicalism of the commandments of the Sermon on the Mount. Here also the great love is required, not only the little one. For inasmuch as God abundantly reveals His love, the love of man also acquires greater possibilities. God's love releases man's love. The love which is from above shatters the callous hearts, frees the prisoners, breaks the ice, and sets love in motion. For it is the love of God's children which is demanded in the Sermon on the Mount. The greatness of this divine love is but partially revealed on this occasion when Jesus spoke to His disciples. The full revelation

took place on the Cross. The commandments of the Sermon on
the Mount should not therefore be separated from the Cross of
Jesus. In their radicalism they are hidden signs of Jesus' own
love. Love towards enemies, love towards the evil and the just,
love to the one and only God, entering the narrow gate — all
these can be called an easy yoke and a light burden (Matt.
11:30), only because Christ Himself first fully undertook the
fulfillment of *this* love which He commands in the Sermon on
the Mount. It is love which can say: "Take my yoke upon you,
and learn of me; for I am meek and lowly in heart" (Matt.
11:29). It is the essential love of God towards mankind. And it
is this fundamentally devotional and sacrificial love which in the
Sermon on the Mount calls forth sacrifice, not only as a gift
which we on our part and in our own power may return; but
as a capacity, a possibility which He Himself establishes in our
lives through *His* love.

*   *   *

However important this insight into the relationship between
the Kingdom of God and good works, and in connection with
this into the radicalism of the Sermon on the Mount, may be,
it does not mean that the problem of the radicalism of the commandments has been solved. In fact, that radicalism has not
even been unfolded in all its sharpness. For we are still faced
with the problem of the practicability of the concrete commandments of the Sermon on the Mount, or rather we are still faced
with the question of the true application and execution of these
commandments. It is in fact on this particular point that we
meet the most divergent views of the Sermon on the Mount.
And this is not surprising, because it is quite natural to ask,
Did Jesus intend that His commandments should be executed
literally and under all circumstances? and what implications are
then involved for the life of the Christian on earth? If he is not
allowed to resist evil, is he then permitted, for instance, to
defend his fatherland in time of war? And if he is to love his
enemies as prescribed by Jesus, is he not without defense against

all manner of arbitrariness and injustice within the community?
Is it then in fact possible to remain in human society?

As the reader is no doubt aware, this concept of the Sermon
on the Mount as a program for social revolution has frequently
been considered as the only possible and proper solution; so,
for example, it was considered by Tolstoi in the beginning of
this century. Later, however, we find it in modified form in various religious and social movements in Europe and in America.
Yet it has never quite gained full admission, because it is not in
accordance with the entire account of the life of Jesus and His
disciples which the Gospels present. Jesus was neither an ascetic
nor a social or political revolutionist. He saw the beauty and
goodness of life and praised it, in the Sermon on the Mount as
well as elsewhere (Matt. 6:29; cf. 11:19). He did not urge sexual
abstinence or poverty. He refrained from a deprecatory judgment of government and courts of law, and accepted them as
indispensable (Matt. 22:21; 5:22). Even as with John the
Baptist, no soldier was required by Jesus to leave his service
(Matt. 8:5; Luke 3:14). Publicans were left at their posts
(Luke 19:2). It is clear that His teaching abounds in illustrations derived from the social and economic life of His day. In
short, though He acclaimed the Kingdom of God above all and
every relationship, even above the most intimate (for example,
Matt. 10:37ff., 16:24ff.), yet it does not follow that He
abandoned or condemned worldly goods, natural relationships,
and social and political institutions. To regard the radical
character of the commandments of the Sermon on the Mount as
ascetic or revolutionary brings one in various ways into sharp
contradiction with the gospel story of Jesus' life and that of His
closest disciples.

Attempts have therefore been made in different ways to find
the answer to this radicalism in the commandments of Jesus.
It has been said that the territory in which the commandments
of Jesus possess absolute authority is a restricted area. Even here
different shades of meaning are discernible.

According to some, these radical commandments are applicable only to distinctly indicated persons. Thus these ordinances would only refer to the public offices (official life) of His *apostles* who should, as proclaimers of the Kingdom, display a radical individual style of living. Even the Roman Catholic distinction between universal commandments, applicable to all people *(praecepta),* and the so-called *consilia evangelica,* applicable only and particularly to the clergy, has been based on the Sermon on the Mount. In this way these radical commandments of the Sermon are limited to the lives of specially qualified persons.

A variant of this conception is encountered in the views of those who consider the commandments of the Sermon on the Mount only applicable to a limited part of a man's life. A distinction is thereby made, in conformity with Luther, between public office and private life. The radical commandments would then apply to private life, to social intercourse, but public and official life would lie beyond the realm in which the commandments of Jesus possess authority. This view is in accordance with the well-known exposition of Luther, who in regard to the underlying problem wrote: "A prince may well be a Christ, but he may not reign as a Christ, and in his reign he is not called a Christ but a prince. His person is in fact a Christ, but his office as a prince stands in no relation to his own Christianity." Thus the Sermon on the Mount and life in the world are severed, as is the Kingdom of God from natural life. As a matter of fact, it is the same separation that Roman Catholic theology makes between the natural and the supranatural, with this difference, that Luther changes this contrast from a physical to an ethical one.

In conclusion, it is necessary to mention in this connection yet another point of view, which has also found adherents in Reformed theology, namely, that the Sermon on the Mount is only destined for the communal life of the Christian Church. In this community one should not swear, nor resist evil, and one should lend without reclamation. But beyond these limits different and other rules are supposed to prevail. According to this view the

Sermon on the Mount is regarded as the law of the Kingdom of God. But that does not imply its validity for secular life. What is suited to the Kingdom of God is not likewise suited to the empires of this world.

*   *   *

In my opinion all these endeavors to limit the extent of the validity of the Sermon on the Mount in order to solve the problem of our Lord's radical commandments are to be rejected, for we do not find any such indication anywhere in the Sermon on the Mount itself. It can never be said that the Sermon on the Mount was intended only for a specific group of Christ's disciples. Jesus Himself testifies to these commandments as the narrow gate and narrow path that leads to life, and says that "not every one that saith unto me, Lord, Lord, shall enter into the kingdom of heaven; but he that doeth the will of my Father who is in heaven" (Matt. 7:21). No one who wishes to enter the Kingdom of God escapes the requirements of these commandments. Neither is it possible to eliminate a particular section of life as not belonging to the sphere of the Sermon on the Mount. Jesus says in fact that even when we find ourselves in a court of justice we are none the less under obligation to His commandments: "Agree with thine adversary quickly while thou art with him in the way [to court]; lest haply the adversary deliver thee to the judge, and the judge deliver thee to the officer, and thou be cast into prison" (Matt. 5:25, RSV). Even as verse 40, Chapter 5 (RSV) states: "And if any man would go to law with thee, and take away thy coat, let him have thy cloak also." Even if these verses are concerned with the people before the judge and not the person of the judge himself, the attempt to separate the official from the personal in the Sermon on the Mount on these grounds must be quite out of the question. Where would the dividing line lie, and whence the leave to dismiss the commandments of Jesus as lying beyond this dividing line?

The same applies to the view that Jesus regulates especially the relationships within the Christian community. The Sermon on the Mount, so to speak, explicitly denies any such idea, because Jesus says: "For if ye love them that love you, what reward have ye? do not even the publicans the same? And if ye salute your brethren only, what do ye more than others? do not even the Gentiles the same?" Hence it cannot be affirmed that the sphere of the validity of the commandments of the Sermon on the Mount can be limited to a particular group of people or to a particular sphere of life without violating the evident purport of the Sermon itself.

To all appearances this places us, however, before a clear contradiction. We are not, to begin with, allowed to confine the radicalism of Jesus' commandments to one particular sphere of life only. On the other hand, we are bound no less to reject the radical-social view of the Sermon on the Mount. What then is the solution to the problem, and what is the character of the validity of these radical commandments?

*   *   *

To come to a clear understanding, it is necessary to make a closer examination of the text of the Sermon on the Mount. What had Jesus in mind with these radical commandments, as they are called, in Matthew 5? Jesus Himself supplies the answer, in verse 17: "Think not that I came to destroy the law or the prophets: I came not to destroy, but to fulfil." Jesus came to fulfill the law. This matter of "fulfilling" refers to Jesus' *teaching* primarily, and not to His *life*. As Calvin remarks: *De doctrina agitur, non de vita*. No new law is given by Jesus, neither did He intend to abolish the law of Moses nor to replace it. His intention is in fact to fulfill the law by His teaching, that is, to demonstrate the true content and purpose of the law.

With this end in view Jesus furnishes in Matthew 5 various applications and illustrations of what the law of God actually demands. This is done in repeated contrast to the Jewish interpreters of the law, who clouded the true and profound sense of the law by their decrees and their capricious interpretations of the law. Jesus claims that the law does not only refer to the external deed, but to the inner disposition as well, that it asks

of us not only love towards neighbors but also love towards
enemies; that appeal to civil law in order to escape the demands
of love is not tolerated; and that one is not only bound to speak
the truth under oath but in all circumstances. All this is explained by means of a number of concrete illustrations and
clear-cut commandments, which again and again give a vertical
cross-section of the law. These illustrations and commandments
aim to show the qualitative significance of the law. He who
endows the Kingdom also takes care that the full demand of the
Kingdom is discerned. Any disciple who is a participant of the
Kingdom is bound seriously to regard the *will* of the heavenly
Father.

At the same time it is clear from the character of the Lord's
commandments as illustrations and examples of compliance
with the law, that the validity of these concrete and separate
commandments can only be clearly and justifiably understood in
relation to the entire revealed law of God. These radical commandments of Jesus represent the radicalism of the *law,* and by
no means something which supersedes the law. The commandments of Jesus may therefore at no time be brought into conflict
with the law, of which they form the illustration and explanation. It is very important to observe this, because the
righteousness as propounded by the law and the prophets, which
Jesus seeks to bring to full recognition, comprises a most com-
pound and complex content. This righteousness does not require
of everyone at every moment and in all circumstances identical
responses. The commandment of love for instance calls for different applications; at times rigid restraint, then again conceding
indulgence. A father who loves his child expresses his love in
different ways, and to anyone paying attention only to external
appearances it may seem as if this father's love is contradictory in
that it concedes and allows, and then again demands and forbids.
It is nevertheless love which impels him equally to the one as to
the other. There are, moreover, different principles in the law
and the prophets which are to be applied only in mutual relation.
The same law commands love as well as justice. Occasionally

all emphasis is placed on inner disposition, then again a correct and external display of obedience is required. This is quite clear to whoever is acquainted with the difficulties of various ethical decisions.

It is worth noting that Jesus did not for a moment exclude this many-sided character of the law nor did He make ethical decision redundant by His radical commandments. While all stress is laid upon the fact that evil should not be resisted and that enemies should be loved, this by no means excludes the possibility that the will and the law of God may in particular circumstances demand that evil should in fact be resisted. Jesus sets the example Himself. He did not, when going forth to be crucified, resist evil, but on other occasions He violently resisted it as embodied in the Pharisees and scribes. In His own act of obedience He appears as a lamb, but He appears also as a lion. This also holds good for the commandments which He gave; these commandments should never be separated from the root from which they spring: the law and the prophets.

We must not, therefore, limit the extent of the validity of the Sermon in any way. The significance of the Sermon lies in the fact that the will of God, as it is revealed in His law, strives to be fulfilled in the full rich sense which Jesus gave that word. On the other hand, we should not give a priori and unrestricted validity to all the *concrete commandments* of Jesus as if He meant to express the entire volume of the law in a few concise commandments. When Jesus says, "Do not swear at all," He is reacting against the practice of His day to distinguish between all sorts of oaths and to give them different values. He says, on the contrary, that whoever loves truth shall put an end to all such sanctimonious casuistry and not swear at all. But this does not mean that He also condemns the pious oath as we find it in the Old Testament; nor does it mean that an oath is permitted before a court of justice but not in the midst of the congregation. Such an inference would be in conflict with the particular character of our Lord's commandments. They are only to be understood truly and correctly in full accordance with the law and the prophets.

The curious *literary* form of Jesus' teaching, to which I referred in the beginning, is also of importance. His teaching is not systematic according to the occidental way of thinking; rather, it is of an intuitive and oriental character. His words have a peculiar paradoxical character; he who has ears, hears them. For this reason they often appear to contradict each other. Compare Christ's words in Matthew 5:16: "Let your light shine before men; that they may see your good works," with those of Matthew 6:1: "Take heed that ye do not your righteousness before men, to be seen of them." This is no contradiction. It is merely two sides of the same matter. Compare also Matthew 7:1: "Judge not, that ye be not judged," with the words of Matthew 7:6, which is also a part of the Sermon on the Mount: "Give not that which is holy unto the dogs, neither cast your pearls before the swine." Taking these statements at their face value, one is compelled to say: Both cannot be true at the same time. If a man should regard his neighbor as a dog or swine and take measures accordingly, surely this means judging. And does not Matthew 7:2 apply here: "For with what judgment ye judge, ye shall be judged"? A man who reasons thus would not have ears with which to hear. He would not understand that the truth and demands of God do not always require similar application in our lives. To make the necessary distinction is what matters. Essentially it is a question of understanding and doing the law of God in all its depth, without the hypocrisy of those who are not inclined to self-denial. And it is towards this end that Jesus exhorts us in the Sermon on the Mount. His commandments indicate the only level on which the will of God in its concrete demands can be understood and can be fulfilled. This level is the level of the Kingdom of God, that is, the degree of love which comes from God and which in the communion with Jesus Christ returns to God.

*   *   *

It is therefore clear, in conclusion, that only such an exposition of the Sermon on the Mount can give us proper insight into the relationship of being a participant of the Kingdom of God and of having the task and the calling of a Christian in this world. Frequently it is maintained that we are dealing here with two different territories. God's Kingdom is thereby presented as spiritual, life on earth as physical. These territories are regarded as being in conflict with each other, as Jesus' commandments in the Sermon on the Mount then in fact prove. These commandments are regarded as forming, in one way or another, a dividing line between the higher and the lower, between grace and nature. Even today this typical contrast still governs the general view of the practical, social, and political life within Christianity. In fact, only one absolute standard is recognized and applied: the law of neighborly love as explained in the Sermon on the Mount. Thus life in its natural ordinations of state and community is actually regarded as belonging to a different order of life.

To my mind such a view of the relationship between God's Kingdom and the world, between the Sermon on the Mount and human society, is in contradiction with the true purpose and significance of the Sermon on the Mount. The maintaining of the natural ordinations together with those which exist because of sin, is not in conflict with the "characteristically Christian" righteousness of the Sermon on the Mount. In fact, it belongs to this same righteousness.

It is noteworthy that Calvin accepts this fact as obvious in his exposition of the Sermon on the Mount. Quite justly it has been observed that Calvin regarded the problem of the Sermon on the Mount not as an ethical but an exegetical one. He gives no general reflections about the relation between the Sermon on the Mount and the life in the world, between the Kingdom of God and daily life, but simply points out in his exposition of Matthew 5 that the validity of Jesus' concrete commandments in the Sermon should be determined in accordance with the divine ordinations for natural life as revealed in the whole Scripture of the Old and the New Testament.

Only this approach, I am convinced, does full justice to the significance of the Sermon on the Mount. There is no contradiction, no difference of level, between Matthew 5 and Romans 13. Kingdom of God does not mean the abolition of God's previous ordinations for the natural and social life. *Gratia non tollit naturam.* There is no antithesis, either, between the principles of the Law of Moses and of the Sermon on the Mount. The latter does not abolish the former, but confirms it. No doubt, the dispensation of the New Testament confronts us with questions quite different from those of the Old Testament. The Kingdom of God cannot be any more identified with God's special care and legislation for only one nation, as in the Old Testament theocracy. Jesus therefore imposed no civil or political law, as Moses did. This, however, by no means suggests that the religious and ethical teaching of Jesus has nothing to do with the life of His disciples amidst the different connections and relationships in the world. On the contrary, social life, political order, international justice as such belong just as well to the righteousness of the Kingdom of God and of the Sermon on the Mount as simple neighborly love. That does not mean that all the concrete commandments of the Sermon are applicable in all circumstances. But it does mean that the children of the Kingdom ought to ask for the Kingdom and God's righteousness in all the sectors of life and that they have to do that in the light of the whole revelation of God to which the Sermon on the Mount refers. In this aspect Calvin shows greater discernment than Luther in his explanation of the gospel.

It cannot be denied, however — and this is my final remark — that the radicalism of the commandments of Jesus is far more directed at teaching us to forsake our temporal life and the properties of this life than to accept and to cherish them. Even to the most excellent and most beautiful which man may receive from God this word applies: "He that loveth father or mother more than me is not worthy of me . . . . He that findeth his life shall lose it; and he that loseth his life for my sake shall find it" (Matt. 10:37, 39). Undoubtedly we find the eschatological motive of the Kingdom reflected herein. The prospect of *celestial* wealth should impel one to forget the *terrestrial,* and to understand that one's rights and duties, one's bread and clothes, yes, each and everything connected with this life, are only of relative value. Of all this Jesus says in the Sermon on the Mount: "Is not the life more than the food, and the body more than the raiment?" (Matt. 6:25). This "more" so necessary for true living lies in the Kingdom of God; and for this reason the Sermon on the Mount is based, from beginning to end, on the concept that whoever has a share in the grace and wealth of the Kingdom must look upon this worldly life in a different and freer way. And the sacrifice which the commandment of God calls for should be brought without hesitation.

Fundamentally it is not an eschatological but a fully religious motive. The radicalism of Jesus' commands in the Sermon on the Mount is not in the first instance based on the concept that life is short, but on the knowledge that God is Lord of all life and that therefore a life not borne by His grace and not existing in surrender to God is a life lost. That is the fundamental meaning of the commandment: "Thou shalt love the Lord thy God with all thy heart, and with all thy soul, and with all thy mind, and with all thy strength" (Mark 12:30). The phrase "with all thy heart" gives the radical commandments of Jesus their application, because God loved the world in Jesus Christ with all His heart. In this way the Kingdom of God is the restoration of life and it is the Sermon on the Mount which indicates the road towards this restoration. It is not opposed to life, to nature, and to the community, but in truth it is for and in support of life. It reveals that the real secret of life does not lie in the nature of things itself, but it lies only in God. Hence this one principle applies to all the commandments of the Sermon on the Mount: "Whosoever would save his life shall lose it: and whosoever shall lose his life for my sake shall find it" (Matt. 16:25). He shall save it in the Kingdom of Heaven, because of the great deeds of God in His Son Jesus Christ.

CHAPTER THREE

THE REDEMPTIVE-HISTORICAL
CHARACTER OF PAUL'S PREACHING

THE WISH TO GIVE a general characterization of the apostle
Paul's preaching may seem unduly audacious. However, what I
have in view is actually more modest. The question is, From
what point of view can Paul's preaching be approached most
adequately? The entrance to this imposing edifice is our concern.
It is clear that there are all sorts of doors leading into it. But
which of these is the main entrance? I cannot, in a small compass, survey all the attempts made in the course of the history of
exegesis to find this main entrance. Still, I should like to mention one or two approaches to this subject so as to make clear
what I mean.

Reformation theology, broadly speaking, found this main
entrance in Paul's preaching of justification by faith. In the
great struggle with Roman Catholic legalism and mysticism the
forensic pronouncements in Paul's epistles to the Romans and
the Galatians were of fundamental significance. Consequently,
the Reformation view of the Pauline epistles was modeled chiefly
on this doctrine of justification. In the case of Luther this is
especially clear. To Luther, Paul's doctrine of justification by
faith in fact became the principium and criterium for his
evaluation of the whole New Testament, as his criticism of the
Epistle of James proves. And, in a sense, subsequent Lutheran
theology went a step further. In it, Luther's struggle to attain
the certainty of faith was re-projected in Paul's conversion on

the road to Damascus. This was also the line of approach to an interpretation of the passage in Acts 9:5: "It is hard for thee to kick against the pricks." In this way Paul's doctrine of justification was placed entirely in the light of Luther's struggle to gain certainty by works. And, accordingly, this furnished the key to understanding the whole of Paul.

In Calvin and in the tradition proceeding from him these matters are probably more balanced. All the same, here, too, justification by faith remains the main entrance. All the other corridors and apartments of the building are, so to speak, connected with it by inner doors. The concept "Christ-for-us" has developed a far greater force in the whole conscious mind of Reformation faith than the Pauline "we-in-Christ." The same judgment would probably be made if the groundwork of the Reformation creeds were analyzed from this point of view. In any case, it seems warrantable to state that in Reformation theology the outlook on Paul's epistles is, strictly speaking, dominated by justification as the principal point of view.

In later exegesis, partly under the influence of the pietistic and mystical decline of the Church, great modifications occurred. Two main trends came to be distinguished: the forensic idea of justification, and the mystical idea of the *Pneuma,* the being-in-Christ. And more and more the stress in the interpretation of Paul shifted from the former to the latter. In the preceding century already, the Tübingen School cleared the road for this. And the great works of Ludemann and Holsten on Paul pointed in that direction. The distinction came to be made between the Jewish and the Greek Paul. The former was said to have expressed the salvation in Christ in the Jewish, legal terminology of justification, satisfaction, and so on. But Paul the Greek, it was believed, thought in such terms as: flesh and spirit, the dying of the old man and the resurrection of the new man. The liberal theologians (such as H. J. Holtzmann, for example) spoke of an evident contrast in the inner structure of Paul's theology. To them the main entrance was manifestly formed by Paul's statements about the Spirit. Not Romans 3 through 5, and Galatians 3 through 4, but Romans 6 through 8 and Galatians 5 constituted the proper entrance. Here lay the way to the mystical Paul of Bousset, Reitzenstein and, partly, also of Deissmann. Not the Old Testament, nor the forensic way of thinking of later Jewry, but the Hellenistic mysteries, the Greek perception of life, was said to provide the clue to the right understanding of Paul. This concept continued into the 1920's and 1930's, and it makes its influence felt until the present day.

One of the most destructive phenomena attending this interpretation of Paul was that the unity of Paul's preaching with Christ's was gradually lost sight of. When indeed Paul is considered as a mystic or a gnostic, in what respect, one may ask, can he still be called an apostle of Jesus Christ? Consequently this concept of the general character of Paul's preaching was accompanied by a breaking of the unity of the New Testament. On the one hand, in this view, Jesus preached the eschatological Kingdom of God, and the original Christian community in Jerusalem, in accordance with this, expected Jesus as the shortly returning Son of Man; on the other hand, however, to Paul the eschatological expectation was scarcely of any real importance. He lived, it was contended, in the consciousness of the vertical proximity of Christ. Jesus was to him the Spirit, and the words of 2 Corinthians 3:17, "The Lord is the Spirit," should thus be looked upon as the most typical statement of the whole of Paul's kerygma.

To my mind all this bears a clear mark of untruth, if only because of the fact that it greatly minimizes the historical and forensic character of Paul's proclamation of salvation. It is evident, though, that we should take up an entirely false problem if we were to consider the pneumatic and the forensic in Paul as two more or less conflicting points of view, and if we were to present the dilemma in such a way that either the former or the latter would secure the actual entrance to Paul's preaching. Surely in Paul himself we perceive nothing of such a tension. For the same reason, however, it may be doubted if one makes one's view really comprehensive enough by continuing to seek the real core of Paul's kerygma in his doctrine of justification by faith. Paul is not only the author of Romans and Galatians, but also — as is to be maintained on historical grounds, too — of Colossians and Ephesians. And here the approaches are rather different from those of the Epistle to the Romans. On what ground, then, can we regard justification by faith as the real starting-point and the only center of Paul's preaching? And, when we do not confine ourselves to the epistles of Paul himself, how can we make sufficiently transparent the intrinsic relation between Christ's preaching of the Kingdom of God and Paul's preaching, if we qualify the latter as the preaching of justification? Is not then the viewpoint of Paul's preaching at any rate rather more restricted than Christ's? These are all questions which, to my mind, deserve serious consideration before we in a traditional way speak about justification as the main theme of Paul's preaching.

*　　　*　　　*

The term "redemptive-historical" (translation of the German expression: *Heilsgeschichtlich*) expresses a new and broader outlook on the general character of Paul's preaching. The question is, however, what is meant by it, and in what way this new approach can offer us any deeper understanding of the inner relationships of Paul's preaching, as well as of the unity between the kerygma of Paul and that of Christ.

The matter itself can perhaps be made clearest when I refer to the obvious difference between Paul and Luther in regard to the significance of justification of faith in their total view on salvation. No doubt, to both justification is of central importance. But in the case of Paul it is part of a much wider relation than in the case of Luther. To Luther justification by faith is the deliverance from a religious crisis. It is to him, before anything else, the reversal of the *ordo salutis* in which he had become mired, namely, of the order of law and gospel, good works and belief in salvation. This reversal in Luther's thoughts was before anything else a personal and soteriological one. And from this new and overwhelming certainty Luther received a new entrance to the Bible, and all other approaches seemed to him to violate the real core of the Scriptures (think of his criticism on the Epistle of James!)

In Paul this is quite different. Before his conversion he had not been mired down at all, as far as he was aware. This clearly appears from his own witness in Philippians 3. The great change of which Paul's preaching bears testimony is not in the first place the reversal in his mind with regard to the *ordo salutis,* but first and foremost with regard to the *historia salutis* in the objective sense of the word. God revealed to him, on the road to Damascus, that Jesus of Nazareth, crucified and persecuted by Paul, is the Messiah sent by God. This is the new, overpowering certainty, that in the crucified and risen Savior the great turning-point in God's times has come. This is the main theme of Paul's ministry and epistles. "Old things are passed away; behold, they are become new" (2 Cor. 5:17). What in very ancient times had indeed been given and promised by God, but which continued hidden, this has now been made manifest, brought to light (2 Tim. 1:10; Col. 1:26; Rom. 16:26). And of this "fulness of the times" (Gal. 4:4), of this *now* of the day of salvation (2 Cor. 6:2), Paul is the herald (Eph. 3:2ff.). The nature of his mission and ministry, therefore, is defined by the history of redemption. He is not merely a religious genius, he is not merely a church reformer, he is a witness of revelation in the original, historical sense of the word. He is the one who, together with the other apostles, is to accompany and explain the penetration of the new aeon into the present time with his testimony.

This viewpoint is of particular importance to vindicate the unity between Paul's kerygma and Christ's teaching of the Kingdom of Heaven. It is a well-known fact that all sorts of contrasts have been said to exist here. But however different the modality in Paul's ministry may be as compared with Jesus Christ's, it can be rightly said that Paul does nothing but explain the eschatological reality which in Christ's teachings is called the

Kingdom. Only, in the case of Paul the emphasis is not especially
on the fact, but on the unthought-of *modus quo* of the fact.
The Gospels make up the imposing overture; the theme of the
New Testament is set therein: This day is this Scripture — the
promise of the great time of Salvation — fulfilled in your ears
(Luke 4:21). Paul as the witness last called stands behind the
facts, notably behind the facts of Christ's death and resurrection.
It is these facts that he is to preach and interpret as the culminat-
ing point of the Kingdom of God which has appeared in Christ,
as the deciding acts in the divine, eschatological drama. The
overture was announced by Christ Himself, and the part of the
evangelists consists in the reciting of the historic course of God's
mighty deeds in the reversal of the times. Paul's ministry represents, substantially, the next phase. It contains the exuberant
response of the Holy Spirit, who begins to explain — after the
work is finished, the angels have returned, and Christ is taken
up from the earth. That is why Paul's preaching is different and
more complicated and more theological than the Synoptic
Gospels. It is as if the Spirit struggles within him to put into
words the sublime spectacle of the rising of the sun of salvation
on behalf of the coming Church. But the unity of what is called
Jesus and Paul is the unity of the great acts of God in the
fullness of the times.

*   *   *

It is at once obvious now, that the central motive of
justification by faith can be understood in its real, pregnant
significance only from this redemptive-historical viewpoint. No
doubt, the *ordo salutis,* that is, the application and appropriation of the salvation, is also involved here. Paul preaches
justification by faith, as opposed to Judaism, and Romans 4 is
the great proof of this. But the starting-point of Paul's preaching
of justification by faith is to be found in the great turning-point
in the *historia salutis.* This is the significance of the great
thematic pronouncement in Romans 1:17, repeated in Romans
3:21: "But now apart from the law a righteousness of God hath

been manifested [from faith to faith—v. 17]." Every word can be used as evidence. "But now" — now that the great day of salvation has become present time, "hath been manifested" — not, in the first place, made known as a noetic piece of information, but has appeared as an historical event. Now the righteousness of God has come to light, without the deeds of the law.

It may be asked: But why is it that in this proclamation salvation is especially indicated as "righteousness of God," that is, as righteousness which is acceptable to God? The answer can only be this: Because this righteousness which God awarded to man represents the salvation of the great future. Righteousness as such is an eschatological gift. That is why Jewry sought for righteousness, that is, for future acquittal in the judgment of God. "Righteousness and life" are together the contents of the messianic salvation. The former is the condition, the latter the purpose of the salvation. But jointly they constitute the contents of the coming time of salvation. And now this is the spectacular thing about Paul's preaching: he proclaims that the righteousness we are trying to acquire and for which we are working with might and main, has become present time already. And it has become so without deeds of the law, exclusively by God's merciful disposal. But this disposal is not just a notification and nothing else. It was the disposal that was accomplished in the drama of His mighty works. It is an historical, not only a noetic notification. For this righteousness of God, this eschatological acquittal, was announced in the death and the resurrection of Christ: "But now, apart from the law a righteousness of God hath been manifested. . . . through the redemption that is in Christ Jesus, whom God set forth to be a propitiation, through faith, in his blood" (namely, on the cross) (Rom. 3:21, RSV) ; "Who was delivered up for our trespasses, and was raised for our justification" (Rom. 4:25) .

So in the great acts of God in Christ's death and resurrection the eschatological gift of justification is breaking through as a reality already present. To Paul the eschatological reality of the divine judgment and the divine acquittal are revealed in the

Cross and in the resurrection of Christ. In this sense he wants to be understood when he says that now the righteousness of God is manifested. And this is the reason why his preaching of the righteousness by faith, too, bears the character of the history of redemption.

And the same holds true for Paul's preaching of the Holy Spirit. Here we touch the discussions about the forensic and the pneumatic character of Paul's ministry. Seen in the light of the history of redemption it is clear that any "either . . . or" is completely meaningless. In Paul's preaching *Dikaiosune Tou Theou* and *Pneuma* are both functioning as the gifts of the great time of redemption, which in the coming of Christ became present time. This holds true for the Spirit in no less an extent than for righteousness. The *Pneuma* in Paul is not in the first place a matter of mystic experience. It may rightly be asked whether the whole notion of mysticism is at all applicable to Paul's preaching. In the whole framework of his ministry the Spirit represents first and foremost an objective reality, namely, that of the new dispensation. That, and nothing else is the sense of the much mistreated statement of 2 Corinthians 3:17: "The Lord is the Spirit." This is not a description of the essence of the *Kyrios,* nor the proof that Paul, as Bousset taught, reversed the eschatological expectation of the original church in Jerusalem into a mystical piety, in which Jesus, the Lord, is nothing but a pneumatic quantity and all eschatology is transposed into mystical experience and ecstasy. The words "The Lord is the Spirit," however, do speak of the *Kyrios* as the eschatological *Kyrios,* the exalted Son of Man, whom Paul is expecting from heaven. For the messianic era is, according to the pronouncements of all prophecy, also the era of the Spirit.

Not the Greek mystery-religions, but the prophecies of Ezekiel and Jeremiah are the background of Paul's speaking and thinking about the Spirit. As such, namely, as the eschatological gift of salvation, the Spirit is the firstfruits, the temporary share, the *aparchē* of the new aeon. At the same time He is the pledge, the *arrabōn* of the entire redemption which the Lord will bring

about. In this way the Lord and the Spirit belong together.
They belong together by virtue of the revelation of the fullness
of time. When the fullness of the times had come (Gal. 4), then
God sent His Son, but together with His Son also the Spirit of
His Son. Therefore, in Paul's preaching the Spirit represents
before anything else the stage of salvation which the Church of
Christ had reached by the coming of the Son.

That is why Spirit is opposed to "flesh." For in Paul flesh, too,
is not primarily an existential notion, but a redemptive-historical
one. Flesh is the mode of existence of man and the world before
the fullness of the times appeared. Flesh is man and world in the
powers of darkness. And opposing this is the Spirit, the *Pneuma,*
not first and foremost as an individual experience, not even in
the first place as an individual reversal, but as a new way of
existence which became present time with the coming of Christ.
Thus Paul can say in Romans 8:9: "But ye are not in the flesh
but in the Spirit." This being in the Spirit is not a mystical, but
an eschatological, redemptive-historical category. It means: You
are no longer in the power of the old aeon; you have passed into
the new one, you are under a different authority. This is the
indicative of redemption, the proclamation of the new state of
life, and it can be followed by the imperative: If we live by the
Spirit, let us also walk by the Spirit. Therefore, too, the relationship between righteousness and Spirit is transparently clear. Not
two competitive motives are brought into play here, not two
types of piety. The forensic and the pneumatic can be differenti-
ated, they can never be separated. The righteousness is condition
of the *Pneuma.* In this respect it precedes. But the righteousness
can also be paraphrased as life itself. That is the reason why
Paul speaks of righteousness of life (Rom. 5:18); that is,
righteousness consisting in life; that is, also, consisting in the
Spirit. What can be analyzed and distinguished here is never
anything but the analysis of the one Christological, eschatological gift of salvation, which was hidden for ages on end, "but
hath now been manifested by the appearance of our Saviour

Christ Jesus, who abolished death, and brought life and immortality to light" (2 Tim. 1:10).

*   *   *

In yet another respect this approach to Paul's preaching is, to my mind, revealing, namely, for an understanding of the appropriation of the salvation thus defined. Here I am thinking particularly of the much discussed expression *en Christō einai* (to be in Christ) and the conception connected with it, which we find again and again in Paul, namely, that the Church has been crucified, has died and has been raised with Christ. Especially on the ground of this phrase *en Christō* and of this conception of having been crucified with Christ, many have thought they could prove the mystical character of Paul's preaching and piety. True, one also finds in Paul the statement that Christ died *for* us *(hyper hymōn)*. In this the other line is supposed to become visible again, namely, the objective, atoning one, which is related to justification by faith. But the expression "in Christ" is of much more frequent occurrence in Paul's epistles. And with this the dominatingly mystical character of Paul's preaching is considered to have been proved.

In Reformation theology these two ideas, Christ-for-us and we-in-Christ, have never been placed in contrast. As a rule one does find the conception here that the latter notion, we-in-Christ, is second in order of time, indicating the spiritual tie between Christ and those who are His. Thus for example in Lord's Day 16 of the Heidelberg Catechism it is first said that Christ died *for* us. Then follows the question: "What *further* benefit do we receive from the sacrifice and death of Christ on the cross?" The answer is: "That by virtue thereof our old man is crucified, dead, and buried with Him; so that the corrupt inclinations of the flesh may no more reign in us. . . ." "By virtue thereof" (or, through His power) clearly denotes that the being in Christ and the having been crucified and having died with Him is here taken to mean spiritual communion, individual existential appropriation of what happened in Christ once, and what He did *for* us.

In this conception it remains difficult for us to see how Paul came to speak in this curious way, namely, of being in Christ and being crucified with Him. Is the apostle using metaphors here? Does he mean that what took place once in Christ is repeated and continued spiritually in those who are His? But how does he come to speak like this? Is this to be explained from an overpowering spiritual experience, a mystical union with Christ, a union enabling him to re-experience, so to speak, this process of death and resurrection spiritually? But it is clear that Paul applies this being crucified with Christ to the whole Church without any exception. Read Colossians 3:1 and verses 18ff. Has this Church, in all its members, the same experience, then? Or, at any rate ought it to know this experience? Every one feels how unsatisfactory a grasp of this concept we are getting in this way. This may be the reason why these expressions have often had something unreal about them to the faith-conscious mind of the Church, and why the Church understands Paul much better when he says: "While we were yet sinners, Christ died for us" (Rom. 5:8), than when he addresses these deep words to fathers, mothers, servants and lords: "For ye died, and your life is hid with Christ in God" (Col. 3:3). This, then, is supposed to represent the mystical, rather inaccessible, sector of Paul's preaching.

It must be questioned, however, if it is possible to distinguish in this way between being-*in*-Christ and *with*-Christ as the spiritual and Christ-*for*-us as the objective. That this explanation does not go very far appears from the fact that Paul not only speaks of being crucified and raised with Christ, but in Ephesians 2:6 he also states that in Christ Jesus God hath made us to sit together in heavenly places. Indeed, he even pronounces in Colossians 3:4 that the Church will come back with Christ. For in this place he writes: "When Christ, who is our life, shall be manifested, then shall ye with him be manifested in glory."

Here the mystical, spiritual interpretation is an utter failure. One must rather say that Paul, when applying to the Church not only the Cross and the death of Christ but also His exaltation until the parousia, is thinking in categories quite different from mystical ones. It is not true that Christ first died *for* those who are His, who only afterwards also die and rise with Him, spiritually, mystically or ethically. No, when He died on Golgotha, they also died with Him, and when He arose in the garden of Joseph of Arimathea, they were raised together with Him. Paul actually says it himself in so many words in 2 Corinthians 5:14: "We thus judge, that one died for all, therefore all died." Consequently, when he says in another place: "For ye died" (Col. 3:3), or, "We who died to sin, how shall we any longer live therein?" (Rom. 6:2), the apostle does not appeal to the conversion of the faithful, but to their being included in Christ's death. And the same holds true for the resurrection, the exaltation in heaven, the coming back of the Church with Christ. Whatever happened to Christ, happened to the Church, not only analogously or metaphorically, but in the historical sense of the word. She was included in Him, was, and is, present in Him throughout all the phases of the great history of salvation.

Here the great power and consequence of Paul's thinking from the point of view of the history of redemption makes itself felt. That Paul can speak about the Church in this way is not on the ground of a certain experience of Christ, but by virtue of Christ's place in the great drama of God's eschatological work of redemption. This is nowhere more apparent than in the parallelism between Adam and Christ. Just as Adam, in his sin and death, represents old mankind, Christ likewise represents, in His death and resurrection, new mankind. In the case of Adam, too, Paul uses the preposition *in*: "For as *in* Adam all die, so also *in* Christ shall all be made alive" (1 Cor. 15:22). Nobody will be prepared to maintain that "in Adam" is a mystical or an ethical formula; the point is that all are *included* in Adam. It is the corporate idea of all-in-one. Thus, too, all are in Christ as the second man, the last Adam. Two "men" are opposed to each other and along with them two aeons and two modes of existence. Being in Adam is the first mode of existence, that of the flesh. Being in Christ the last, the eschatological mode of existence, always taking it in the corporative sense, that is, of the One, and of all included in Him. Thus mankind is in Adam, and the Church, the predestined Church, in Christ.

"In Christ," therefore, is not a mystical formula; it is a redemptive-historical formula, it is an ecclesiological formula. And it is from this vantage point that the whole transfer of the Christological history of salvation to the Church becomes clear. The phrase "in Christ" sheds its light all around, backwards, in the middle, and forwards. Thus it can be said that the Church has been elected in Christ (Eph. 1:4), because Christ has been elected and her faith in her election is her faith in Christ. Being in Him, she is also in the Spirit (Rom. 8:9). For being in Christ implies both, the forensic as well as the pneumatic. Because the Church is in Christ, *His* resurrection is *her* justification, already in the garden of Joseph. But therefore she is also "in the Spirit." For the redemptive-historical sequence is not: Christ, Spirit, Church; but rather, Christ, the Church in Christ, Spirit. Therefore faith and Christian life can only derive their power from this all-embracing "in Christ." And therefore, too, are Paul's own exhortations nothing but one great application and one mighty appeal to this being "in Christ."

Of course, at this juncture one may ask: "How does Paul come to this concept of the oneness of all in One?" Historians of religions try to clarify this in all sorts of ways. Some even want to hark back to Iranian (Persian) religions to retrace the idea of the *anthrōpos,* of primeval man. We do not need to look that far, I think. What Paul expresses in this way is nothing but what the Old Testament itself presents in various ways, namely, that in the great future the Messiah, or by whatever other name He is called, *represents* the people of the future. The same truth finds expression in the messianic title, the Son of Man. In Daniel 7, the Son of Man represents the people of the saints of the Most High, and consequently He is hardly distinguishable from

His people in this prophecy. Indeed, when Jesus Himself says in the gospel that the Son of Man came to give His life a ransom for many, and when at the last supper He gave them His body and blood for food and drink — this rested on the same unity between the Messiah and His people. We may say that Paul comes, *post factum,* to an explication of this unity, which is unequaled in all that had been said before him. For now it has appeared in the process of redemption as revealed in Christ, that this unity consists in a unity of Cross and death, of resurrection, of heavenly citizenship, of being made manifest in glory. This is no ecstasy and no mysticism, this is no speculative theology, this is the explication of the history of salvation. This history, and this only, enables the Church to conceive the breadth and length and height and depth, and to know the love of Christ, which surpasses knowledge, that the Church may be made full with the fullness of God.

*   *   *

I have only indicated some main facts. When the anthropological and ecclesiastical aspects are considered in more detail, it appears how much the total structure of Paul's gospel is dominated by this main thought, how everything has, so to speak, been arranged within this one, great redemptive-historical framework. Then it also appears how much the epistles to the Romans, Ephesians, Galatians and Colossians form a unity; indeed, how the great cosmic perspectives of Colossians 1 and 2 cannot be missed here either. One more question presents itself: What implications has this view of the Pauline kerygma for the continued ministry of the Church? This is really a new subject and therefore I shall confine myself to only a few remarks.

First. Our concern is a way of approach. In a sense the contents of the preaching of salvation are outside our scope. The great central concepts such as justification, life, liberty, and grace do not change their contents. But the way of approach, the general viewpoint, the access to the Pauline kerygma still remains of great importance. When the general viewpoint is too narrow, the stresses in the preaching will also change, the choice of texts will be reduced and certain sectors of the Pauline kerygma will remain, for the Church, in the dark, and the great relations, notably those between Christ's and Paul's preaching, will become blurred. It seems to me that it is right to ask whether the Reformation preaching from the epistles of Paul always escaped these faults, and whether such preaching is avoiding them now. Of course, all this cannot be dissociated from the tradition of the Reformation in which we have taken root, nor from the arrangement of our Reformation creeds.

It may seem ungrateful to speak critically about Reformation preaching. For if the truth of God was ever adequately maintained in the face of the destructive inroads of human legalism, it was in the Reformation confession by the Pauline plea: The just shall live by faith without deeds of the law. But precisely this antithetical position of the Reformation confessions against Roman Catholicism can explain why the forensic, and not the eschatological, character of the gospel has left its mark on the Reformation soteriology. It may be said that this position was the only possible and admissible one to adopt. But it cannot be said that the exegetical and homiletic approaches to Paul's epistles must forever be thus determined. If they are, the stream of revelation will be channeled quite too much in the traditions of the Church.

Second. If asked what the functioning of this wider approach to the Pauline kerygma could mean with respect to preaching in our day, I would reply: It can be a mighty support for us in the present crisis of certitudes. In Reformation times, too, a life and death struggle was carried on, with the ultimate certainties of the Church at stake. Today that crisis is perhaps even deeper and more fundamental. Then the question was whether man shall be justified by faith or by works. It was then that the Pauline kerygma of the justification by faith saved the Church. Now the issue is whether man in general has any need of justification at all. The question is presented whether truth and certainty can be found anywhere except in the true existence of man himself, and whether truth is not simply subjectivity and no more. Thus the whole history of salvation is thrown into the crisis. It is more than mere accident that in our time the battle about the existentialist interpretation of the gospel overlaps for the greater part that of the demythologizing of the facts of salvation. Put in a simple way, the issue is whether this history of salvation is something more than what takes place in man himself. And this issue concerns not only theologians and philosophers. With ever increasing force it is required that the preaching of Christ should make clear to man how he is existentially concerned in the gospel. And the criticism of preaching is largely bound up with this, although most people may never have heard of Kierkegaard, Heidegger, or Bultmann.

Now this demand that preaching should bring home to man his being concerned in the gospel, is a decidedly legitimate one. But it is also a dangerous one. For great is the temptation for the preacher to approach this involvement of man and gospel not from the gospel but from man. When the approach is made from man, then it is no more the analysis of the history of redemption in Jesus Christ which reveals the real existence of man, but it is the analysis of man in his actual situation which serves as the criterion for what is acceptable in the history of salvation. In this crisis of certitudes, in this struggle of the being or not being of the Church, the gospel of the apostle Paul can once more save the Church from destruction. The apostle preaches the gospel in a really existential way. He preaches not only the facts of salvation which once have happened in the history of Jesus Christ; he also points out in an incomparable way man's concern in God's beneficial deeds in Christ Jesus. For he places man in the facts of salvation, man in Christ, in His death and resurrection, in His ascension into heaven, and consequently man in the Holy Spirit. But this means that for the knowledge of man in his real existence as well as for his salvation there is no other way and possibility than in what once has happened in the history of Christ. This history reveals the very existence of man in its distress and in its redemption. And it is only in the involvement in this history of salvation, in the death and glorification of Christ, that the existence of man can be saved and has been saved.

Third. Paul knows and preaches not only about the existence of man in Christ but also about the possibility of man's being outside Him and outside the salvation. For the existence of man is included in Christ only in so far as it is included in His body, that is, in His people and in His Church. And Christ's body reveals itself in the belief of those who belong to it. Therefore the preaching of the gospel in the sense of Paul is no mere proclamation of the history of salvation and of man's concern in it; it is, too, a mighty exhortation to faith. Paul, the great herald of the history of redemption, is at the same time the passionate preacher of faith as the gate, the only gate to this redemption. He has a passion for Christ, and therefore a passion for souls, that he may induce them to faith. And from the contents of the Pauline gospel the very nature of faith can become clear, as well as the separation faith makes between man and man. That faith is the belief that God has dealt with me in Christ and therefore will deal with me also. It is the faith that knows itself and the world, that knows life and death, because it knows all things in the light of the coming of Christ, in the revelation of His hiddenness and in the hiddenness of His revelation, until time comes when even the history of redemption will no longer know a tomorrow.

CHAPTER FOUR

THE LAW OF GOD IN PAUL'S DOCTRINE OF SALVATION

ONE OF THE most important subjects in the history of New Testament revelation is the position occupied by the law in the Pauline teaching of salvation. We have seen in our discussion of the Sermon on the Mount that Jesus ascribed an altogether positive, and at the same time radical, significance to the law and the commandments of God in His teaching. Is this true of Paul?

This is an interesting question — and not only from a purely instructive point of view, because quite a profound discussion rages on this problem, in exegetical as well as ethical literature. How did Paul stand in regard to the law? It is well known that a number of truly negative pronouncements on law are to be found in Pauline writings. For this reason many claim that Paul regarded the law in a purely negative sense. In terms of this viewpoint gospel and law would stand in opposition to each other as representatives of the two aeons. The law would represent the old and unsaved world; the gospel on the other hand the era of Christ and of the Kingdom of God. That would mean the termination, once for all, of the law.

The question arises, then, of the relationship of Jesus to Paul. When, for example, the Sermon on the Mount greatly stresses compliance with the commandments, as we believe we are able to maintain, is it then at all possible to speak of a unity between Jesus and Paul? Are we not confronted with a profound difference between the Gospels and the epistles of Paul, because in the former all stress is laid upon the positive meaning of the law, and in the latter upon the negative meaning? Does not Christ fully emphasize righteousness according to the law, while Paul is primarily the preacher of righteousness without the works of the law? Is it therefore possible on adequate grounds to construct a harmony of Matthew 5-7 and Paul's epistle to the Romans?

To this problem a number of ethical questions have to be added. Of primary importance is the question of the so-called *tertius usus legis* (or "third" use of the law). It is a well-known fact that the *tertius usus legis* was less prominent in Lutheran theology than in Calvinist. In subsequent development this distinction has become even more pointed, especially in some Lutheran theologians in Scandinavia, who strongly resist any emphasis other than the negative one upon the law in the order of salvation. In Luther's more humanistically inclined followers the entire concept of law, as externally applied authority, is regarded as contraband. To them not the law but the Spirit is the principle of knowing God's will. This Spirit would realize itself in the human will, in the Christian autonomy. All endeavor to maintain the law as the principle of the knowledge of God's will is branded as legalism and rigid adherence to the *letter* of the law. In its place appeal is made to Christian freedom, Christian right of self-determination and Christian conscience. And this appeal is made in the belief that it accords with Pauline teaching, even if the objective bystander receives the impression that in this way Immanuel Kant has greatly replaced the apostle Paul.

In our exposition we shall try to make an approach to the question from an exegetical point of view.

Of what significance is the law to Paul? What is the freedom of the law, which he discusses with such great preference, especially in his Epistle to the Galatians?

*   *   *

To give the problem its proper setting, it is necessary to see that the subject of the law is broached in Paul's letters especially in regard to his struggle against Judaism. For the Jews of his day the law, as given to Israel, was the great ray of light in the complete darkness of the human race. The law was Israel's glory and privilege; it was her real possibility of receiving life. The following saying stems from Hillel: "Where much flesh is, are many worms; where much treasure is, many cares; where many women are, great superstition; and where much law is, there is much living." Israel did in fact receive the law from God as an exceptional privilege, by which she was to acquire life itself. Therefore did Israel boast in the law. It was her means of laying up treasures in heaven, her merit before God. Possession of the law distinguished Israel from the Gentiles. Romans 2:17 (RSV) is a typical example of the sense of superiority which the Jews fostered by virtue of their possession of the law: "You call yourself a Jew and rely upon the law and boast of your relation to God and know his will and approve what is excellent, because you are instructed in the law, and . . . you are sure that you are a guide to the blind, a light to those who are in darkness, a corrector of the foolish, a teacher of children, having in the law the embodiment of knowledge and truth. . . ."

It is true, however, that we also find a consciousness of sin in Judaism. In general, it was conceived that every man sins. Of Rabbi Gamaliel II it is said in the Talmud that when he read the severe demands of the law in Ezekiel he wept and cried: "Whoever complies with all, he is justified, but alas, not he who executes only one of these commands." This notion, however, never drove the Jew to despair of the law. The Jew lived by a quantitative interpretation of the law. His fulfillment of each individual requirement of the law indicated merit, no matter how small. The root of his soteriology existed in the conception that if his fulfillments of the law quantitatively resulted in victory over transgressions of the law, he would be justified before God. In this system no one could be confident of the outcome. Only at death was the account of each drawn up, the credit and debit postings made. For this reason the law-abiding Israelite was advised to regard himself, at every moment of his life, as a half-justified and a half-sinful man. It was his duty continually to endeavor to turn the scales in his favor by merit. In this state of affairs he could hope, but not know, that he would be justified and acquitted before God in the final day of judgment.

It is in this sphere of thought that Paul lived, boasted and relied on the law, until he was struck as if by lightning on the road to Damascus. He refers to it in his Epistle to the Philippians (3:4-6, RSV): "Though I myself have reason for confidence in the flesh also. If any other man thinks he has reason for confidence in the flesh, I have more: circumcised on the eighth day, of the people of Israel, of the tribe of Benjamin, a Hebrew born of Hebrews; as to the law a Pharisee, as to zeal a persecutor of the church, as to righteousness under the law blameless."

In these words we hear something of an echo of the former Pharisee. So had Paul lived, too. What diverted him from this road? Did he lose faith in his own justification? Did he fail to find peace, despite his ardent zeal? Paul himself tells us differently. It was the great discovery that God revealed Himself to the world in Christ and that He revealed a different and hitherto unsuspected road to justification. From this revelation, from the Cross of Christ, did the light break forth on the imperfection and incompletion of that which he formerly held in such high esteem: "But whatever gain I had, I counted as loss for the sake of Christ. Indeed I count everything as loss because of the surpassing worth of knowing Christ Jesus my Lord. For his sake I have suffered the loss of all things, and count them as refuse, in order that I may gain Christ. . . ." (Phil. 3:7, 8, RSV).

A different justification presented itself to him, which abolished the one by which he had lived previously, a righteousness not of his own, based on law, but that which is through faith in Christ, the righteousness from God, which depends on faith. Henceforth Paul was led to a different view of righteousness than the one he previously held, namely, a righteousness based on the law. Paul did not gain knowledge of Christ and the Cross by virtue of his knowledge of man. Quite the contrary: the knowledge of Christ, the surpassing worth of His Cross, presented him with true knowledge of man lost in his sin and delusion.

In this way Romans 1 through 3 is to be understood. It is the knowledge of Christ which causes him to speak thus. Only now does he see the fancy of the boasting Pharisee, now does he see the qualitative meaning of sin, which prevents all possibility of obtaining justification and life in the way of the law. Not only are the heathen, because of their debaucheries or because of their little knowledge of the law, unable to find salvation, but the Jews themselves, in spite of all their knowledge and privileges, cannot find righteousness and life. Not the hearers of the law are righteous before God, but the doers of the law will be justified. And the fulfillment of the law does not exist in a quantitative accumulation of special good works, but in the qualitative obedience to the law as the will of God and the commandment of love.

Therefore the apostle does not hesitate to apply to every man the Old Testament verdicts upon the evil and godless: "None is righteous, no, not one; no one understands, no one seeks for God. All have turned aside, together they have gone wrong; no one does good, not even one" (Rom. 3:10-12, RSV). And therefore, too, he can quote these words as a proof that the law does not give acquittal and life, but even condemns every man: "So that every mouth may be stopped, and the whole world may be held accountable to God. For no human being will be justified in his sight by works of the law since through the law comes knowledge of sin" (Rom. 3:19, 20, RSV).

Although Paul's doctrine of the law has only partly been called to attention, it is possible even at this point to intimate a general and preliminary conclusion. In this radical conception of sin and law there exists a profound agreement between Paul and Jesus. In regard to the contents of the law and the qualitative judgment thereof, Paul takes stand with Jesus in profound contrast to Judaism. Even if the contents of the law are not so fully and consistently explicated by Paul as they are by Jesus, in the Sermon on the Mount for instance, one is nevertheless justified in saying that Paul's conception of the law is in full agreement with that of Jesus. Paul, too, reduces the entire contents of the law to the requirement of love (Rom. 13:8-10; Gal. 5:14; 1 Cor. 13). He refers to it predominantly in the singular and not seldom in personifications (Rom. 7). Hence it may be concluded without hesitation that Paul's rejection of the law as a means of grace is founded on the same profound view of sin which occupies such a dominant position in the teaching of Jesus on the law. In this respect, at least, there is a complete harmony between Christ's and Paul's teaching.

*   *   *

With that, however, not everything has been said of Paul's doctrine of the law. The most characteristic point is that Paul not only rejects the law as a means of grace, but that he also attains to a thorough understanding of the significance of the law for the sinner. One should always remember that Paul, as a devout Jew, boasted in the law as a means of obtaining everlasting life. But now, through Christ, it was wrenched from his grasp. Obviously the question should arise: If no one fulfills the requirements of the law, or is able to do so, to what purpose did God impose the law? (Rom. 3:31; 7:7,13, and elsewhere). As a result of this question Paul attains to his far-reaching exposition of the place occupied by the law in the history of redemption.

Wholly typical of the Pauline conception of the law is the fact that Paul on more than one occasion speaks of the law as of *secondary* importance, for instance in Romans 5:20, where he says: "law came in *besides*," and in Galatians 3:17,19: "the law . . . came four hundred and thirty years *after*," and "it was *added* because of transgressions." The law, according to this view, is a new and supplementary measure of God. Initially God gave His promise, His guarantee of redemption to Abraham. Later, four hundred and thirty years later, the law was added thereto. This fact does not mean that the promise which God once made to Abraham could be broken or be made conditional. The law was added because of transgressions, and this addition involves what Romans 5:20 asserts: "that the trespass might abound." This evoking of transgressions lies not only in the result, but, in a sense, as surely in the purpose of the law. The law provokes sin, for sin shoots forth like a bright flame when the law is applied to forbid it. Sin properly manifests itself in its very nature whenever the law raises its voice. Paul discusses this fact in a remarkable way in Romans 7 (RSV): "Our sinful passions [were] aroused by the law" (v. 5), and further on in the same connection: "What then shall we say? That the law is sin? By no means! . . . But sin, finding opportunity in the commandment, wrought in me all kinds of covetousness. Apart from the law sin lies dead. I was once alive apart from the law, but when the commandment came, sin revived. . . . For sin, finding opportunity in the commandment, deceived me and by it killed me" (vv. 7-11).

Here Paul, in express terms, asserts that the law "aroused" and "wrought" sin and that sin takes the law as its "opportunity." Sin may even be called "dead" without the law, which is to say that the virulence of sin only fully works out itself when it comes into contact with the law. Then does the law wring out all manner of desire and release its full fury against the power which seeks to curb it. What is said in 1 Corinthians 15:56 also applies here: "The power of sin is the law." Without the law sin would not have been able to incite man to such resistance and revolt. Hence it may be said that sin deceives man. By presenting the law as the terminating point of all freedom, of life itself, sin brings man under its bewitching power. It promises him the very things of which the law seems to deprive him and thus leads him to death. This effect of the law on sinning man is what the apostle has in mind when he announces that the law increases sin (Rom. 5:20), and that sin by way of the commandment becomes sinful beyond measure (Rom. 7:13). Because sin takes hold of God's commandments to induce man to transgression, its true character is exposed and becomes alive only by the law of God. This is a necessary and indispensable result. And this is the function which Paul again and again ascribes to the law in God's purpose, to provoke and manifest sin.

*   *   *

In these terms it is clear why the apostle repeatedly describes the law as a power which threatens man, deprives him of his freedom and takes him into its custody. No doubt, sin is the great supposition to all this. Yet the opposing force and menacing power against man is not only attributed to sin but also to the law. The law constitutes a prison in which man lies captive; a jailer who guards him. "But now," claims the apostle in Romans 7:6, "we have been discharged from the law, having died to that wherein we were held." This reflection is especially prominent in Galatians, where he says: "Before faith came, we were confined under the law, kept under restraint" (3:23, RSV).

Paul also describes the law as the pedagogue, or the custodian: "The law was our custodian until Christ came. . . . But now that faith has come, we are no longer under a custodian" (Gal. 3:24,25, RSV). Pedagogue here means not so much an educator as a guardian of minors. The *tertium comparationis* consists not, positively, in the education, but, negatively, in the lack of freedom for as long as man is under custodianship. This is evident enough in Galatians 4:1,2, RSV: "I mean that the heir, as long as he is a child, is no better than a slave . . . he is under guardians and trustees until the date set by the father."

In all these illustrations the law stands between man and his freedom. It keeps him in bondage and in captivity under a strange power, as appears from the contrast in Galatians 4:4,5: "But when the fullness of the time came, God sent forth his Son, born of a woman, born under the law, that he might redeem them that were under the law." "To be under the law" — an expression frequently recurring in Paul's epistles (Rom. 6:14,15; 1 Cor. 9:20; Gal. 4:5,21; 5:18) — signifies quite clearly the contrast between being under a hostile and enslaving power and being under grace (Rom. 6:14) and living in freedom.

Because of all this Paul frequently describes the Christian era as the date from which the law lost its claim on man. "Ye are not under law, but under grace" (Rom. 6:14), and again, "You have died to law through the body of Christ, so that you may belong to another" (Rom. 7:4, RSV). A few other important passages may also be mentioned: "But if ye are led by the Spirit, ye are not under the law" (Gal. 5:18); "But now that faith is come, we are no longer under a tutor" (Gal. 3:25); and the most far-reaching of them all: "For Christ is the end of the law, that every one who has faith may be justified" (Rom. 10:4, RSV).

The endeavor has been made to translate "end" in Romans 10:4 by "aim" (purpose), in order to maintain that Paul did not regard the coming of Christ as the terminating of the law in an absolute sense, but rather that the law only then received its due appreciation. "Object" or "purpose" is then taken to mean that the law, in a positive way, directs attention to Christ, for example, in its sacrifices and various ceremonies. In the same sense, the law is regarded as our pedagogue, custodian, to Christ.

To me, however, this point of view appears to be excessively governed by doctrinal considerations. When Paul describes the law as a custodian in Galatians 3, the whole context indicates that he does not assign the law a positive and pedagogical, but a negative and enslaving, meaning (see above). It is apparent that even in Romans 10:4 Paul neither refers to the law as the entire revelation of the Old Testament, nor as the ceremonies which foreshadow the Messiah. The law as reflected in this passage really represents "personal" righteousness, the principle: "Do this and you will live." For this reason the translation by which Christ is indicated as "the end" of the law is, in my opinion, indisputable. Christ is hereby not represented as the hidden content of the law, but on the contrary as One who stands opposite to the law and who brings the law to its end.

*   *   *

In the light of what has been said, the meaning of Paul's negative evaluation of the law is no longer obscure. Paul, it should be remembered, is taking a stand against the Judaistic interpretation of the law, namely, as means of salvation. In regard to this, whatever he says about the law may be summarized in one single sentence: Whoever expects his salvation by way of the law will be deceived. He will not survive by means of the law, but he will be condemned by it; he will not be given life, but deprived of it. Paul does not, however, regard the law *in itself* as a force hostile to man. Paul expresses himself quite clearly on this point: "What then shall we say? That the law is sin? By no means. . . . The law is holy, and the commandment is holy and just and good. Did that which is good, then, bring death to me? By no means! It was sin, working death in me through what is good" (Rom. 7:7,12,13, RSV). Nevertheless, the law became a power hostile to man *as a result of sin*. For the power of sin is the law (1 Cor. 15:56). The law is bilateral: it acquits the righteous, but condemns the sinner. And because Paul here completely regards the law from a Judaistic point of view, namely, as means of salvation, he is unable to speak of the law except as a slaying, enslaving, and menacing power.

This thought he develops not only in forensic, but also in psychological-existential categories. Not only in a forensic sense does the law bring down a curse upon sin, and not only is the sinner threatened by the eschatological sanction of the law, but the law constitutes also an enslaving power, in the ethical and existential sense of the word. Herein lies the profound significance of Romans 7. The law has an adverse effect upon the sinner in that it in no way improves him but rather causes his degeneracy. This is said in an absolute sense, and it is thus said because Paul so accurately discerns the true character of sin. As sinner, man is able, to a certain extent, to meet the requirements of the law, but only for as long as he allows sin a certain amount of moving space in his life. When the law enters, however, to oppose sin quite radically, sin is aroused; and opposition against the law increases. Then only does man become true sinner by means of the law. Then also does he die, that is, he is subjected in his entire existence, forensically and ethically, to sin. For this reason Paul often uses *sin* and *law* as synonyms (Rom. 6:14: "For sin shall not have dominion over you: for ye are not under law, but under grace"). When man is "under law," sin has dominion over him. Then is the law the principle by which he lives. But he is unable to live by that principle, and he dies as a result of it. Sin achieves dominion over him. For this reason grace exists not only in dying to sin but also in dying to or before the law (Rom. 7:4; Gal. 2:19). The dying is a dying to the law as means of grace, and therefore also a dying to the sanction, the claim, which the unfulfilled law imposes on man.

Only from this point of view, the profound, negative conclusions on law are to be understood, even when Paul contrasts law and the Spirit, as in Galatians 5:18: "If ye are led by the Spirit, ye are not under the law." This contrast occurs frequently in Paul: "The letter killeth, but the Spirit giveth life" (2 Cor. 3:6). This contrast does not imply, however, as is often concluded, that the law as written code inadequately expresses the contents of righteousness, and that man should steer only by the compass of the Spirit in order to know the will of God. Of such a modern posing of the problem Paul is quite ignorant. No, when he says that we are not under the law but under the Spirit, he has in mind that we are no longer dependent upon the law in regard to the *fulfillment* of righteousness, or the *doing* of God's commandments. Rather, we are dependent upon the Spirit. The unregenerated man hopes to live by the law, but the law, the letter, the written code kills. The law is unable to confer life (Gal. 3:21); it is powerless because of sin (Rom. 8:3). What the law cannot accomplish, however, the Spirit can. The Spirit not only commands but also renders man capable of doing what is required. Therefore the dispensation of the Spirit stands in contrast with the dispensation of the law, as the dispensation of righteousness and life stands in contrast with the dispensation of condemnation and death (2 Cor. 3:7ff.). Such is Paul's conception of the law, a conception which completely inverts the Jewish boasting in the law as means of grace. It is a contemplation of the law in its competitive relationship with the Cross and the Spirit of Christ.

It is, moreover, a remarkable fact that Paul not only describes this significance of the law as the actual consequence of the functioning of the law in a sinful human world, but that he also indicates quite clearly that this operation of the law is included in the divine administration of salvation. For God thus prepared the way of Christ: "The scripture [that is, God] consigned all things to sin, that what was promised to faith in Jesus Christ might be given to those who believe. Now before faith came, we were confined under the law, kept under restraint until faith should be revealed. So that the law was our custodian *until* Christ came, that we might be justified by faith" (Gal. 3:22-24, RSV). In the light of these remarks it is clear that for Paul the law did not constitute a power beside God and Christ, to threaten and destroy man. Even in its enslaving and slaying action the law has a preparatory meaning. The law is given in order that the way to life and freedom may be revealed more distinctly. It is unable to violate the power of the promise given to Abraham, but by its condemning and slaying ability it obstructs and blocks every road other than that of the promise.

*   *   *

Although in this way the law has an unequalled position in the history of revelation, the question remains: To what extent did Paul consider the law to function positively, in distinction from its negative function? To put the question differently: From the Pauline point of view, does the purport of the law in the divine plan of salvation consist only in the *usus paedagogicus* of the law?

The answer to this question is of great importance not only with regard to the relationship of Jesus' and Paul's views of the function of the law, as has already been indicated, but also with regard to the significance of the law in the Old Testament. It frequently seems, when reading Paul, as if the dispensation of law means nothing else than the dispensation of death and condemnation, and as if the law in all its aspects represents the former aeon, the age of the world and of the flesh. If we read the Old Testament, however, we notice that the law primarily and functionally rests on the foundation of grace as the principle of the covenant between God and His chosen people (Ex. 20:2). To mention but one example, Psalm 119 sings the praise of the law as the privilege which the pious of the Old Testament knew to possess, and for which purpose they continually summoned God's help and aid. Should we now, because of Paul's negative pronouncements, take it for granted that Paul did not notice this positive meaning of the law, its functioning in the Old Testament on the basis of grace, and that he also saw no place for the law in Christian life, after the advent of Christ?

A most radical point of view in this regard is sometimes found in orthodox Lutheran theology. According to this theology, Paul assigned the law no other than a preparatory meaning, and his various comments on the law, in terms of which we are freed from the law, should therefore be understood in an *absolute* sense. Paul's conception of the law leaves, in this view, no room whatsoever for a *tertius usus legis* (third use of the law). This view is defended with great determination by the Swedish Bishop Anders Nygren in his very valuable commentary on Paul's Epistle to the Romans.

This point of view, however, which is also found in a number of other commentaries in more or less explicit form, is pressed by the objection that the apostle, along with his apparent absolute judgment of the law as negative, in more than one passage describes the law as the continuous demand of God on both believer and unbeliever. The important passages in this regard are: "For God has done what the law, weakened by the flesh, could not do . . . in order that the just requirement of the law might be fulfilled in us, who walk not according to the flesh but according to the Spirit" (Rom. 8:3,4, RSV); "Owe no one anything, save to love one another: for he who loveth his neighbor hath fulfilled the law. . . . love therefore is the fulfillment of the law" (Rom. 13:8,10); "To those outside the law I became as one outside the law — not being without law toward God but under the law of Christ" (1 Cor. 9:21, RSV) ; "For the whole law is fulfilled in one word, even in this: Thou shalt love thy neighbor as thy self" (Gal. 5:14) ; "Bear ye one another's burdens, and so fulfill the law of Christ" (Gal. 6:2) .

Some writers have endeavored to bring these passages into agreement with the exclusively negative view of the law by saying that love as the fulfillment of the law also makes the law superfluous. This is, however, clearly an argument resulting from embarrassment. Paul does not describe love as the termination of the law, nor does he assert that love makes the law superfluous. He speaks of love as the fulfillment of the law, a fulfillment which is demanded from the believer and which supposes the continuous commandment of the law.

Others have endeavored to distinguish in Paul between the law as eternal and everlasting will of God, which prevails in every believer by way of the Spirit, and the law of Moses, which was done away with by Christ. But when Paul discusses the permanent demand of the law and indicates it more specifically and in concrete form as love, he says in fact that this is the fulfillment of the ten commandments (Rom. 13:8-10) , that is, fulfillment of the law of Moses. To repudiate the so-called third use of the law in Paul's teaching is therefore not possible without resorting to capriciousness and artificiality. The weight of Romans 13:8-10 and Galatians 5:14 is unmistakable. The love mentioned in these passages does not function in Paul's epistles as a new Christian ideal which replaces the law; rather, it is in fact the fulfillment of the law. It is also untrue that the law henceforth finds its criterion in love; rather the contrary: that which the demand of love implies and which makes this demand so imperative is to be found in the law. It is therefore impossible to oppose this lasting, authoritative meaning of the law both from the point of view of Paul's Christology and of his pneumatology.

It is true that Paul considers the law in 1 Corinthians 9:21 as such that he may be said to be "under the law of Christ." Likewise in Galatians 6:2 he uses the expression "the law of Christ."

And some maintain that the words of Romans 13:8 should not be translated by: "he that loveth his neighbor hath fulfilled the law," but by: "he that loveth hath fulfilled another [the other] law." This "other law" then refers to "the law of Christ," which distinguishes it from the law of Moses. In my opinion this translation of Romans 13:8 is unacceptable. The fact remains, however, that Paul, in 1 Corinthians 9:21 and Galatians 6:2, specifically connects the demands of the law with Christ. Christ is not only the medium of the fulfillment but also of the contents of the law.

Of however great importance this may be for the correct understanding of the continual demand of the law, we should nevertheless not regard it as a substitute formula for the purpose of indicating the contents of the law. Undoubtedly not all the requirements of the law of Moses continue to be authoritative after the coming of Christ. However, despite the fact that Paul strongly opposes those who desire to tie the true believers among the Gentiles to circumcision and all manner of ceremony and ritual prescription (Gal. 2:14; Col. 2:16, and elsewhere), it does not alter the fact that he uses the Mosaic law not only summarily, but that he also appeals to it concretely (Eph. 6:2,3). It is not possible to find in Paul's extant epistles, in express terms a criterion by which we can discern what is no longer valid after Christ's advent, and what remains valid for the future. The apostle gives no systematic arrangement; he merely poses and presumes a fact. From his Christological point of view Paul does not abolish the law as the expression of the will of God, but rather he upholds it.

What is true of Paul's Christological utterances about the law is also true of his pneumatological utterances. Quite definitely the possibility of *doing* what the law requires lies in this that true believers are in the Spirit and live through the Spirit (Gal. 5:25). The fact remains, however, that the work of the Spirit consists in working out the law of God in the life of the believers (Rom. 8:4). Therefore we do not find in Paul's epistles a spiritualistic way of thinking, which, in regard to the *contents*

of the will of God, makes a contrast between "law" and "Spirit,"
"external ordinance" and "internal disposition." To Paul it is
quite evident that the norm of Christian life is in the law as an
expression of the will of God. Only in this way is it possible to
explain why Paul in his Epistle to the Galatians, for instance, in
which he makes the sharpest pronouncements about the negative
significance of the law, nevertheless, without further explanation,
declares that love is indispensable because it is the fulfillment of
the law. Only the Spirit can arouse the love, and without the
Spirit the law is powerless as a result of the flesh (Rom. 7:13-25;
8:4). However, the law as good and holy commandment is not
suspended by the Spirit. It is the Spirit who writes the law in
the hearts (2 Cor. 3), and the fruits of the Spirit are the good
works which the law prescribes.

And so, too, the expression "freedom of the law" in the
Pauline epistles is explained. It is the freedom of the law as
vital principle without Christ and without the Spirit. This
principle works condemnation and death. Christian freedom
therefore means freedom from the condemnation and death
which the law works without Christ. It means acquittal from
God's judgment; it means, even here and now, a good and
sanctified conscience. It means, moreover, the freedom, the possibility, to live with the aid of the Spirit in agreement with God's
demands as expressed in the law. It is the freedom, moral freedom, to do what God requires. There can be no greater error
than using Paul for an appeal to the autonomy of Kant, even if
the latter is interpreted in a Christian way. Christ, the Spirit,
and love form a unity in Paul, and therefore Christ, the Spirit,
and the fulfillment of the law are not to be separated.

It may be said that the most characteristic of Paul's expressions
on the law are not to be found in Romans 13 and Galatians 5,
but in Romans 7 and Galatians 3. In these chapters the great
contrast with Judaism prevails. In them we see Paul as the great
witness of the Cross of Christ and the accuser of man in his
delusion. Because of this contrast and this testimony Paul's
viewpoint may appear one-sided, but he became the great leading

power of the Church through all ages by his struggle against all that glories in the flesh. He became the great teacher who reveals man in the hidden chambers of his heart and in his having been sold under sin. Paul is, nevertheless, a disciple of Christ in the full sense of the word, which is to say that he is not only witness to the Cross of Christ but also witness to the commandments of Christ. The anthropological and redemptive-historical way of approaching the law in Paul's doctrine is, therefore, not in conflict with the words which Jesus uses in His requisitory against the Pharisees: "Think not that I came to destroy the law or the prophets: I came not to destroy, but to fulfil" (Matt. 5:17). The servant is not above his Lord; Paul is merely preparing room for his Master in order that the Lord Himself may fulfill the law and the prophets, in the life of His congregation, too.

Such, and none other, is the profound meaning of Paul's doctrine of the law, and in it all he is verily an apostle and witness of Jesus Christ the Lord.

CHAPTER FIVE

HISTORY OF REDEMPTION AND THE SCRIPTURES OF THE NEW TESTAMENT

IN THE PRECEDING expositions we have dealt in some detail with the Kingdom of God in its historical manifestation in Christ Jesus. And we have also tried to understand, particularly from the epistles of Paul, what the salvation of the Kingdom of God implies for the Church. The question that finally presents itself as a logical sequence is: Where can we find assurances that this historical revelation of God in Jesus Christ actually happened in this way; and where can we find the certainty that what thus happened really has been explained in the right way — in Paul's kerygma, for instance?

Here we are facing the question, again widely discussed in our time, of the relationship between the history of redemption and the Scriptures of the New Testament. For we have no other sources revealing all this to us than the books of the New Testament. Do these, however, give an adequate picture of what once happened? Are they historically reliable? And does the explication of the great facts of salvation, as found in Paul for instance, accord with the intention of Christ Himself? What guarantee does the Church possess in this respect? What guarantee does she have that she does not live by the fallible word of man but by the infallible word of God?

At present the most wide-spread concept within the Christian Church is that in Christ Jesus God has revealed Himself to man, but that the writings of the New Testament are merely the human report of this, a report which undoubtedly may be of outstanding value, because these men lived very close to the great events of salvation and still reflected in their writings some of the powerful impressions which Jesus made on His contemporaries, but a report nevertheless which is human from beginning to end and not more than human. This is the position also adopted by many so-called orthodox theologians. Recently someone put it as follows: "There is much solid talk about the deeds of God in Christ Jesus as subject to no doubt whatsoever. But the recording of this in the Scriptures is discussed as a purely human matter."

There are also other views, of course. The view of radical biblical criticism, which rejects not only the divine character of the Scriptures but also of the history which they set forth, is still alive. And this criticism asserts itself anew with great vigor. Here the German scholar Rudolf Bultmann is the guide to many. In his view the historical Jesus completely disappears from sight. The virgin birth, the resurrection, the miracles are myths; the content of the Gospels is the theology which the early apostolic church built up around Jesus. It is all very important but only as the witness of the *faith* of the first Christians, and not as the witness from true history. Paul and John, too, are criticized radically. Their concepts about the Logos, about the Savior who descended from heaven, about the cosmic significance of Christ, are looked upon as a syncretism of Christian beliefs and pre-Christian gnosis. The task of Christian theology is supposed to consist in discovering the enduring hard core in these mythological and gnostical ideas.

With respect to all this criticism of the Scriptures, whether moderate or radical, one question remains: In what way do the critics think that they can still hear the word of God in the Gospels? For it is their claim that they remain faithful to the Scriptures. In this human, all too human witness, full of errors and myths, full of historical and theological corruption, we nonetheless hear the word of God, they assert.

In this area of theology, as well as in other areas, the great influence of the Barthian conception of Holy Scripture is making itself felt. Although in many respects himself a champion for the contents of the Holy Scripture against radical criticism, Barth nevertheless refuses to accept the Scriptures and the word of God as identical. Scripture *is* not the word of God, but it must *become* the word of God again and again. Scripture is the auditorium in which we are to listen to God, but it does not follow that when we sit in the auditorium we hear God speak. That depends upon whether God is speaking, whether He makes His voice go forth. God's word is not enclosed in this book of narratives and epistles. Only when God sends forth His Spirit does this word of men turn into the word of God.

In my opinion we are here confronted with a spiritualistic concept of the word of God. Now one may add the remark that Barth nevertheless wants to maintain the historicity of the great facts of salvation, and of the miracles, and the preaching of Jesus as unimpeachable and holy. In my opinion, we have to notice that with thankfulness. But it is not clear how Barth thinks he can theologically justify himself against the radical criticism, for instance, of such as Bultmann. For the latter, too, likes to speak much of the word of God, the kerygma shining forth from Holy Scripture. Only, Bultmann connects his belief in the word of God with a much more radical criticism of the New Testament. What Barth accepts as unassailable history, as for example the resurrection of Christ, Bultmann declares a myth. What Bultmann finally retains as the contents of the word of God is an exhortation to an existential decision. The fact of salvation as recorded in the Scriptures, and the New Testament preaching of Jesus and Paul are not to him the word of God; rather, that is the word of God which in these Scriptures calls man in his concrete situation *hic et nunc* to liberty. The curious situation we are facing today is that in European theology a struggle has broken out between Barth and Bultmann which, one may say, is implacable, and that the issue is generally the significance of the historical dealings of God in Jesus Christ, but that still in this controversy Bultmann with his radical criticism can in a sense use Barth's own conception of the word of God.

If the Scriptures as such are not the word of God, and if man must rather hear the word of God in them again and again, is any appeal to the Scriptures against radical criticism then at all possible?

Here the great problem of the so-called orthodox Scriptural criticism becomes manifest: on the one hand this criticism will give free scope to historical criticism, while on the other it draws back halfway. On the one hand it will not dissociate faith and the historical fact of salvation; yet on the other it is not prepared to recognize the Scriptures in their recording of these facts of salvation as historically unimpeachable.

The Reformed concept of Scripture has, from old times, laid all its stress on the authority of the Scriptures as the word of God. It does not allow man to make a qualitative distinction between the Scriptures and the word of God, and it refers to the self-evidence of Holy Scripture in numerous passages. Therefore Reformation theology has spoken of verbal inspiration, and it does not allow a separation to be made between the literal and the theological exegesis of the New Testament.

This position is a very strong one against all sorts of subjectivism; and I think it becomes increasingly clear that without this principle of the Scriptures as the expressed word of God — I do not say that without it no belief is possible, for the authority of the word of God is stronger than the criticism of theology! — there is no possibility of sufficient theological resistance against subjectivism in its various forms and against the assaults upon the absoluteness of the Christian faith. Without the principle of Scripture as the expressed word of God there is no sufficient defense against the existentialist interpretation of the great facts of salvation. And in *its* turn, the existentialist interpretation of the word of God is, without this principle, unable to give an answer to the remarkable question which the unbelieving philosopher Karl Jaspers laid before Rudolf Bultmann, namely, on what grounds does Bultmann think that the transcendental gift of freedom can only be found in the listening to the historical Christian kerygma in the Scriptures and not in another way.

All this can be a strong argument in favor of the indispensability of the appeal to the Scriptures as the expressed word of God. On the other hand it is clear that faith in the Scriptures as the word of God can never be a mere postulate required by the insolvable problems of the criticism of the Scriptures. What we need is a clear insight into the organic connection between God's dealing in the history of salvation and His speaking in the Scriptures. In this respect, I think, there is something more that ought to be said than usually has been said so far, even in Reformed theology. The organic unity of the faith in Christ and the faith in the Scriptures as the Word of God is not always as clear as it should be. Therefore I think it is not superfluous to investigate the connection of God's revelation in Christ and His revelation in the Scriptures in more detail. To my mind two things are at stake here: first, the authority of the New Testament itself; and second, the nature of this authority.

*   *   *

The first thing I should like to stress as being opposed to the spiritualistic and actualistic conceptions of the word of God is the fact that in the very core of the history of salvation Christ Himself has taken care of the account and tradition of what happened in the fullness of time through an authorized institution. From the beginning of His appearance Christ has allowed men to participate in His own authority, or *exousia*, in order to give this authority a permanent and concrete form for the foundation and the preservation of His Church on earth.

Especially the institution of *the apostolate* should be mentioned here. Nowadays we know that the notion of apostleship has its origin in the field of Jewish law and justice. The figure of an apostle, or, as the Jews had it, of a *schaliach,* is a man who is entitled to appear and to act on behalf of another man. The Jews said: The *schaliach* (apostle) of a man is as much as the man himself. Hence it is a phenomenon of special importance that Christ Jesus surrounded Himself, from the beginning of

His public ministry, with a circle of disciples, and gave them instructions as apostles. We may ask, What was their task and what was their place in the history of revelation?

The answer is that they are the foundation of the Church because they are ear- and eye-*witnesses* of the *magnalia Dei* in Christ Jesus, especially of His death and resurrection. All the statements in the Acts of the Apostles which prove this could here be quoted, as for instance Acts 1:8: "Ye shall be my witnesses both in Jerusalem, and in all Judaea and Samaria, and unto the uttermost part of the earth."

We must distinguish between the apostle and the witness. Not all witnesses of what has happened are apostles. Not all of them are qualified and authorized to speak in the name of Jesus Christ. The witness of the apostles has the authority of Jesus Himself. The apostles participate in His mission; they are, together with Him, the rock, the foundation, the pillars of the Church (Matt. 16:18; Eph. 2:20; Gal. 2:9; Rev. 21:14). But they are this because upon their witness to the great acts of God in Jesus Christ the Church is built.

Especially important in this complex of thoughts is Christ's word to Peter: "You are Peter, and on this rock I will build my church, and the powers of death shall not prevail against it" (Matt. 16:18, RSV). For Peter is the rock because of his confession, "You are the Christ." But not only this general confession is meant here. The foundation of the Church in the person of Peter is connected especially with the powers of death. This is the significance of Peter for the Church of the future, that he (and the other apostles) guarantee the Church its unassailability from death. It is clear that neither Peter nor the other apostles are able to preserve the Church from death. When, in spite of that, Peter is called the rock of the Church, against which the powers of death are powerless, it is because Peter and the other apostles represent the certainty of resurrection. They are the rock and foundation of the Church because of their witness to the resurrection. In Matthew 16 this point is still made in veiled words. But before long Peter himself declares that the ministry of the apostleship consists before everything else in the witness to the resurrection of Christ. And as such, as a witness to the resurrection, the apostleship is the rock of the Church.

These few data may suffice to show that in the New Testament itself the central events of salvation are closely connected with the authorized proclamation and the tradition of the apostles. The records of salvation cannot be separated, as merely human, from the history of salvation. The recording, the tradition, is not left to chance, nor to the common tradition, nor to the believing community. It belongs first and foremost as apostolic preaching to the reality of revelation itself.

Another characteristic description of the same matter can be found in Hebrews 2. Here the significance of the apostles in the history of revelation is compared with the task of the angels in the Old Covenant. The message declared by angels — this is the purpose of Hebrews 2 — was valid *(bebaios)*. In the same way the New Testament salvation is first declared by the Lord and after that "attested as valid" to us by those who heard Him, the apostles. They are not only witnesses or preachers in the ordinary, ecclesiastical sense of the word. Their word is once for all the witness for Church and world in the forensic sense. They are the witnesses *a parte Dei et Christi* for all times to guarantee the reality and to explain the significance of the great acts of God in His Son Jesus Christ.

*   *   *

In this connection we have to mention the work of the Holy Spirit in the apostolic ministry. The election of the apostles is at once assigned to the Holy Spirit. We read in Acts 1:2 that Jesus was taken up, after He had given commandment to the apostles whom He had chosen through the Holy Spirit. And it is the same Spirit who enables the apostles to fulfill their ministry. Especially the statements in John 14-17 are of the greatest importance in this respect. The witness of the Spirit and the witness of the apostles are very closely related. "The Spirit of truth . . . will bear witness to me; and you also are witnesses, because you have been with me from the beginning" (15:26,27, RSV). The witness of the Spirit is not entirely a thing other than the witness of the apostles, but it finds its expression in the witness of the apostles. For the Spirit will not speak on His own authority, but whatever He hears He will speak; and "He shall take of mine, and shall declare it unto you" (16:13-15). The same thought is found in 14:26 (RSV): "The Counselor, the Holy Spirit . . . will teach you all things, and bring to your remembrance all that I have said to you." The Spirit of God is the teacher and guide of the apostles. But His work is not to be understood apart from the witness of the apostles. He takes care of their witness. And this is why their witness becomes His witness. This does not mean that in spite of the fallibility and weakness of the human witness the Holy Spirit would nevertheless use it for His own purposes, but it means that the Spirit would enable them to speak and to write the witness of the Spirit. To say it in dogmatic terms: In these Johannine statements all stress lies on the *testimonium Spiritus Sancti externum.*

There is more to be said in regard to the apostolic witness. The New Testament speaks again and again about *tradition.* Let me bring only a few passages to mind. In the first chapter of Luke we read about what is "delivered [*paredosan*] to us by those who from the beginning were eyewitnesses and ministers of the word" (1:2, RSV). And the Epistle of Jude speaks of "the faith which was once for all delivered [*paradotheise*] to the saints" (v. 3, RSV). The best-known *paradosis* passage we find in 1 Corinthians 15:1-3 (RSV): "Now I remind you, brethren, in what terms I preached to you the gospel, which you received [by tradition, *parelabete*]. . . . For I delivered to you [by tradition, *paredoka*] as of first importance what I also received [by tradition, *parelabon*], that Christ died for our sins in accordance with the scriptures." Most commentators hold that in all these sayings tradition has a secular, general meaning. The apostle Paul, too, is supposed to quote in 1 Corinthians 15 a more or less fixed creed of the Christian community. The New Testament concept of tradition is considered to be in accordance with the common laws of human traditions. And so, according to this view, we should look upon the whole New Testament witness as a purely human tradition of the revelation of God.

But it is certain that this concept of tradition *(paradosis)* is not the concept the New Testament writers themselves have of tradition. The Jewish background of this concept proves that the tradition about which Paul and Luke are speaking is not in the first place of a social nature and does not have its *Sitz im Leben* in the collectivity of the Christian community. It represents an authoritative, personal institution, that is, the institution of the apostles. This is evident from 1 Corinthians 15, where Paul lists the apostolic eye-witnesses who guarantee the truth of the tradition. Tradition in the New Testament view is only another word for the authoritative preaching of the apostles. Tradition is identified with the teaching to which the community has to submit in obedience. Tradition is the word of God (1 Thess. 2:13) which the community heard from the apostles and which they accepted not as the word of men but as what it really is, the word of God.

Paul speaks about tradition in the full consciousness of his apostolic authority. And he can do so because he knows that Christ the raised and exalted Lord stands behind this tradition. In 1 Corinthians 11:23 (RSV) he says: "For I received [by tradition, *paralebon*] from the Lord what I also delivered [by tradition, *paredoka*] to you." It is clear, I think, that Paul does not speak about an immediate revelation of the Lord, nor about an oral communication in the past. What he means is that the tradition he has received as an apostle, and which he has delivered to the Church, is a holy tradition, the tradition in which the Lord Himself speaks to His believers. Therefore the tradition in the New Testament is part of the revelation and of the history of revelation itself. It is the word of the living Lord, it is the authoritative word *concerning* Christ and the word *of* Christ.

It is the truth that has been entrusted to the apostles and through their ministry by the Holy Spirit (2 Tim. 1:14).

*   *   *

Space would fail me if I were to trace throughout the New Testament what may be called the canonicity of the apostolic preaching, the apostolic witness, the apostolic tradition. This canonicity is not the stamp which the Church put on the tradition. It is the canonicity which Jesus Christ Himself conferred on His apostles. Therefore the later recognition of the apostolic writings and apostolic preaching as canon is neither to be considered as a *testimonium paupertatis,* as a proof of the poverty of the later Church, nor as a mere defensive measure against heresy, but first and foremost as the recognition which the Church gave and had to give to the authorization of the apostles of Christ, to their endowment with the Holy Spirit, and to the promise of the Lord: On this rock I will build my Church.

I realize that not all the problems of the canonization of the New Testament have been solved. But the key to the solution of the whole problem of canonization and the authority of the New Testament Scriptures is the recognition of its Christological basis. Jesus Christ is not only the canon Himself, in which God comes to the world, but He also lays down the canon and gives it a concrete, historical shape in the authority of the apostles, in their witness and tradition. And He guarantees the connection between this authoritative institution and the Church: On this rock I will build my Church.

The question may be asked on what grounds we can be sure that our New Testament and the authority of Christ, given to the apostles in a qualitative sense, might be identified. It is not possible to give here a full treatment of that question. But two things should always be kept in mind: (1) The Church had been built upon the established, apostolic tradition long before problems of canonization arose; and (2) these problems were never concerned with the great and main contents of the later canon of the New Testament. About these there never was any hesitation or uncertainty.

When we realize what urged the Church to recognize that established apostolic tradition as norm, rule, and standard, no other answer can be given than this: Why do you recognize two particular persons as your father and mother? It is the certainty that I was born of them. The Church never made the canon. The Church accepted and recognized it because the Church knew she was born of it and was built on that rock. If anyone asks, How do you know that the Church is not built on a foundation other than that which Jesus Christ has laid?, I cannot say anything but this: It is the a priori of my belief *in Him*. If Christ has laid the foundation of the Church in the apostolic ministry and has promised to build the Church upon this rock, and if the Church never had a foundation other than the tradition which is established in the Scriptures of the New Testament, then I cannot believe that the foundation of Christ and the foundation of the Church are two different things.

This is the Christological a priori of my faith in the apostolicity of the Church, this is also the Christological a priori of my faith in the Scriptures of the New Testament. The Scriptures of the New Testament are not only the instrument by which Christ and the Holy Spirit build the Church in their divine, unsearchable, and inscrutable way. No, the Scriptures of the New Testament themselves are normative and authoritative for the Church. They participate in the event of revelation not only *hic et nunc,* not only when and if God will convert them into His Word, but they are revelation in the historical and definite sense of that word. In their established, Scriptural, and literal form they participate in the authority of Christ and the Holy Spirit. And the apostolicity and Christianity of the Church depends on the recognition of that authority.

*   *   *

From this point of view it is, I think, possible to distinguish a little more precisely the nature of the authority of the Scriptures of the New Testament. My point is to stress that the authority must be approached from the history of revelation and salvation itself. The nature of this revelation defines also the nature of the Scriptures and their authority.

The authority of the Scriptures has often been approached apart from their historical character. It is possible to make a theory of inspiration in which not the nature of the Scriptures themselves, but our theological postulates about what inspiration ought to be define the concept of the authority and the inspiration of the Scriptures. It is possible to think that the Scriptures are books of divine oracles, every word or sentence of which contains a revealed or hidden divine truth about all sorts of things. In the history of exegesis we find the allegorical interpretation of the Scriptures; we also find the dogmatic interpretation. Each interpretation has its own particular concept of inspiration and revelation. The presupposition of the dogmatic interpretation, for instance, is that the Scriptures are the treasure-house of dogmatic *loca probantia,* which we only have to put together and to bring into a system in order to acquire biblical dogmatics. To such a concept of the Scriptures and the inspiration of the Scriptures we must not raise the objection that it stresses the revelational character of the Scriptures too much. Rather the objection must be that in this way the nature of the Scriptures and of revelation in general is not sufficiently distinguished, and that the historical character of revelation has been lost sight of.

To return to our subject proper: What is the nature of the Books of the New Testament and from what point of view are we able to discern their essential character and authority? For an answer we must look to their contents, that is, to the very nature of the revelation of God in Christ. And what is the nature of that revelation? What is its scope and aim? Is it to bring knowledge to men in the widest sense which the word has? Is it to reveal all the mysteries in heaven and on earth? Is it to give us a supplement to our general knowledge of the past? Is it to give us a detailed account of the events in the future? And is it, then, our task to read Holy Scripture from this point of view and to seek its authority in the several regions of human knowledge?

Here we have to remember all that has been said previously about the content of the New Testament revelation. Its real content is the coming of the Kingdom, the coming of the great time of salvation. Its content consists of the great acts of God in His Son Jesus Christ. Therefore the essential nature of the New Testament Scriptures is first and foremost that of a *proclamation*. The standard expression for that idea is *kerygma* or *euangelion*. When the Gospel of Mark opens with these words, "The beginning of the gospel of Jesus Christ," we should hear in the word "gospel," *euangelion,* the note of actuality. It means: The beginning of the apostolic proclamation of the great time of salvation. And the word *kerygma* that we meet again and again in the New Testament has the same meaning.

This definition of the original meaning of the Gospels is important as a hermeneutic principle. It can help us to obtain an adequate appreciation of the Gospels as historical writings. It is known that scholars have for a long time made an attempt to come to what is called a life of Jesus, that is, an historical picture of the person and the experiences of Jesus comparable to the biographies of other great men in history. In the course of these attempts it has become more and more evident that the Gospels are very imperfect books of history. It is not possible to acquire a real insight into the historical succession of all the recorded events. The Synoptic Gospels do not give us an exact account of place and time for all the occurrences in Galilee. The sequence of the words and deeds in the Gospel of Matthew is in many cases very different from that in Mark and Luke. We do not receive any information as to the duration of the appearance of the Lord in Galilee. And what are we to say of the differences in construction and scenery between the Synoptic Gospels and the Johannine Gospel? The result of these studies about the life of Jesus has been that the criticism of the Gospels has steadily gained strength, that the historical value of the Synoptic Gospels has become, in the estimation of many scholars, of a very dubious nature, and that the Gospel of John has more and more been considered to be a book of a theologian and to be without the slightest historical importance.

The heyday of this kind of criticism belongs to the past, and the true nature of the Gospels is more clearly realized again. The scope of the Evangelists differs widely from that of the common writer of history. They do not claim to give an accurate and continuous report of the history of Jesus, but to show in what way the Kingdom of God had come in Him. For their purpose it was not important to give an exact account of all the journeys that Jesus made, nor to make known on precisely what occasions Jesus spoke all His words. It is very likely that they did not even know themselves, their sole object being to hand down the kerygma of the salvation in Jesus Christ to the Church and to the world. They were not notaries, they were not distinguished historians, they were preachers of the gospel of Jesus Christ, proclaimers and heralds of the fulfillment of God's promises in His Son.

* * *

I know that here the danger of separating history and kerygma is imminent. All existentialist theology of the New Testament is kerygma-theology. The most important representatives of this theology say: We do not know what has happened; there is no certainty about the historical Jesus, no certainty as to what happened in the garden of Joseph of Arimathea, no certainty whether Jesus made the claim to be the Messiah. As history books the Gospels are unreliable. Only in the kerygma of the Gospels do we find the word of God. And it is that kerygma which speaks to us and becomes for us the word of God again and again. It is the kerygma that we have to repent and that we have to decide *against* our securities and *for* the possibility of the Holy Spirit in our lives. This means Kingdom of God, and this is why Jesus is our Lord and Messiah even if He Himself never pretended to be.

It is obvious that this interpretation of the word *kerygma* is the reversal of the gospel. Undoubtedly the gospel is kerygma; it is not a mere annal of historical events; it demands our decision. But the crucial question is whether the historical facts as reported in the Gospels are decisive for human existence. Bultmann and his pupils say: The history of those facts is uncertain. The kerygma only becomes history *(Geschichte)* when it brings man to his real and true existence. I am convinced that this influential interpretation of the kerygma is the reversal of the gospel of Jesus Christ.

Here again we have to mention the word *witness*. For kerygma and witness, as qualifications of the contents of the gospel, always go together. And witness means that what is witnessed is something visible and audible. A witness of Jesus Christ in the original sense of the word is a man who bears witness of what he has seen and heard to friends and foes alike. And the New Testament notion of witness can never be divorced from these contents. This is in full harmony with the very nature of the gospel itself. Its main theme is God acting in His Son Jesus Christ, when the time for such acting had fully come. Therefore any attempt to separate the kerygma and the history of salvation in Jesus Christ is the corruption of the gospel.

For that reason the authority of the Scriptures of the New Testament also implies their historical reliability. But the relation between kerygma and witness is a mutual one. For not only does the kerygma depend on the witness, but, conversely, the witness has its aim and scope in the kerygma. The concept of witness *(marturia)* in the New Testament has a pregnant and two-sided sense. Never is it a mere historical witness; it is always a witness that appeals to faith. It is the witness of facts, and at the same time of the truth *in* the facts. In the later books of the New Testament, for instance in the Gospel of John, this second aspect is most conspicuous.

This explains very largely the form of the Gospels. I have already pointed out that the Gospels are not historical books in the accepted sense of the word. This also applies to their witness-character. The witness of Christ's words and deeds is always a witness from — shall I say — this theological viewpoint. This accounts for many features of the Gospels which viewed otherwise bring us into difficulties with regard to the authority of Holy Scripture. When we read the Synoptics carefully we encounter all sorts of uncertainties. We notice that the words that Jesus spoke on a particular occasion are recorded in various forms, as for instance the beatifications in the Sermon on the Mount, the institution of the holy supper and perhaps the Lord's prayer. We find one evangelist using and altering the order and form of the sayings and narratives of another evangelist. We cannot always harmonize all the details in the three Synoptic Gospels.

What about this fact? What about the authority of Holy Scripture? What about verbal inspiration? I am under no delusion that I can speak the final word in this matter. If anywhere, here we should be eager to learn the Spirit's own concept about His work and to beware of prescribing our concepts to the Spirit of God. The books of the New Testament are the word of God to His Church by the inspiration of the Holy Spirit. That means that God expresses Himself and addresses us in the words and the letters of the Holy Scripture. This means verbal inspiration and we need not fear that in the formation of the Scripture some things have escaped the supervision of the Holy Spirit. But this is not to say that the Spirit would give us a literal account of all the words and deeds of Jesus Christ. The Spirit has inspired men, has inspired the apostles, according to the promises of Jesus Himself, in order to be the foundation of the Church. And the Spirit has guided them in such a way that their words and writings are the foundations of the Church. This is the infallibility of the word of the Scriptures as the word of God. We can rely on their witness as a kerygma to the faith in the *magnalia Dei* in Jesus Christ.

It is possible that some people require more. They would make such an arrangement of the Gospels that they could make a fine map of all the journeys of Jesus, know how many months

He wandered in Galilee, tell precisely how many blind men there were at Jericho when Jesus passed, one or two, possess all the words of Jesus in their literal form — not only in Greek, but in the language in which Jesus spoke them.

It is a fact, however, that the witness of the apostles and the witness of the Spirit do not have such a nature. It is the witness about that which can be expressed thus: "These are written, that ye may believe that Jesus is the Christ, the Son of God; and that believing ye may have life in his name" (John 20:31). This was what I meant when I said in the beginning that the authority of the New Testament writings is included in the nature of these writings.

*   *   *

Thus far we have treated the Gospels in particular. There are, however, more books in the New Testament and the question can be asked if we can qualify all the other books, too, as kerygma and as witness of the *magnalia Dei* in Jesus Christ. The real subject of Paul's preaching was, as I have pointed out before, the announcement of the new times in Jesus Christ, the revelation of what was hidden. This is the same as what in the Gospels is called the coming of the Kingdom. As a matter of fact, the epistles of Paul are in the wider sense of the word, kerygma, *euangelion,* of and about Jesus Christ, proclamation of what God did when the time had fully come. The witness-character, too, is not missing. I have only to remind you of 1 Corinthians 15 to make this clear. Nevertheless, the modality of Paul's kerygma is different from that of the Gospels. We can characterize it as the explanation of the history of salvation which is recorded for us in the Gospels. For that reason Paul's epistles, and the greater part of the remaining books of the New Testament, have rather the character of teaching, that is, doctrine (the New Testament says: *didache, didaskalia*). The contents of the kerygma and the *didache* in the New Testament are exactly the same, but the modality is different. What is proclaimed by the herald is explained by the teacher. So we can understand that what in the opening of the New Testament is

called the kerygma of the Kingdom of Heaven, in the later parts
assumes a different shape, that of religious teaching and doctrine.
I have only to mention the Epistle to the Romans. It is a doctrine of the history of salvation; it is in its character doctrine,
not kerygma in the original sense of the word.

This distinction is very important. It can help us in regard to
the irrationalistic trends in the interpretation of the New Testament. It shows us the authority of the New Testament from
another point of view. The Christian faith is not just a belief in
facts, but also a faith in the significance of facts. The task of the
apostles was not only to preach and to bear witness, but also to
teach. In that respect Paul especially has been the apostolic
teacher *par excellence* of the Church. This teaching, as well as
the original kerygma, belongs to the foundation of the Church.
The belief in what happened when the time had fully come is
also knowledge, *gnosis* and *sofia*. This does not imply that the
New Testament gives us a complete system of truth. The New
Testament is not a theological book, and the answer we have to
give to its teaching is not in the first place a theological, but a
religious one. The New Testament teaching calls for faith and
obedience, not primarily for scholarship and theological erudi-
tion. But one cannot say that there is faith without teaching and
knowledge. Christian faith is not only a new method of life, it is
also a new knowledge of life, of man, of history, of time, of the
future, and of the world.

On the other hand, we have always to distinguish the real
nature of the revelation of the New Testament and, in accordance with it, the nature of the authority of New Testament
teaching. Paul's epistles, to restrict ourselves to these, teach us
many things but always teach us from one central point, namely,
from the cross and the resurrection of Christ. These wonderful
epistles comprise in a certain sense all things in heaven and on
earth; they contain, if I may use this word here, an all-embracing
philosophy. But their revelatory character consists in the fact
that they place all things in the light of the great works of God
in His Son Jesus Christ. In the description of these acts of God

the apostle uses the language and the concepts of a time that has gone. He speaks in anthropological and cosmological terms which we can often hardly understand. We have a concept of the cosmos different from the tripartite one: heaven, earth, and what is under the earth. We can scarcely understand his concept of flesh *(sarks)* and mind *(nous)*. Here the problem will remain how far we can and may distinguish between word and reality, Scripture and revelation, between the concept of the matter and the matter itself. Here we are up against the great and important hermeneutic question: What is the teaching of the New Testament, what is the intention of the Holy Spirit? The authority of the New Testament cannot be expressed in one word. We have to approach it from the real nature of the New Testament revelation: the kerygma, the witness and the teaching of what God did in His Son, when the time had fully come. From this center the light beams forth all around, illuminating the history and life of man.

The Scriptures of the New Testament bear their authority because they are not mere human writings but because they have a contribution to make to the coming of the Kingdom itself. They are the rock on which Christ has built and will continue to build His Church, in accordance with the very nature of the revelation of God in Christ Himself. From this point of view we are to approach and to believe them and to preserve them as the prophetic, infallible word of God, a lamp shining in a dark place, until the day dawns and the morning star arises in our hearts.

INDEXES

INDEX OF SUBJECTS AND PERSONS

INDEX OF SCRIPTURE